Dating Backward

A practical guide to dating and finding your soul mate.

By

Rick Soetebier

and

Penny Dunning MSN APRN FNP-BC

ISBN: 1492817880

ISBN 13: 9781492817888

Library of Congress Control Number: 2013919134

CreateSpace Independent Publishing Platform,

North Charleston, South Carolina

Table of Contents

Acknowledgments

Rick Soetebier

First and foremost I want to thank God for leading me down a most amazing path. He has granted me wisdom and discernment that have been key for me to be able to follow His guidance to take the journey I am now on. In spite of all the mistakes I have made in life, He loves me enough to keep nudging me in the right direction. The wisdom and discernment He has granted me have allowed me to see the next step of His vision for me. Do I know where this path will lead? Absolutely not, but I am confident that I am where He wants me right now.

Next I want to thank my best friend, Dr. Ron Massie. He has been a friend to me for at least fifteen years. Over that time our friendship has grown to a level like no other that I have known. He has been an encourager, a confidant, a sounding board, the brother I never had, and a brother in Christ. He has been there for me during my darkest times. Many times he has let me rant and rave about my problems of the day or reveled in my daily joys and victories. He always knows what to say, but more importantly he also knows when to say nothing at all. My hope is that I have been able to be half the friend to him that he has been to me.

My ex-wife, Toni, taught me many life lessons and has been a significant part of my life's journey. Many of these life lessons have helped form the foundation for who I am today and the basis for developing some of the lessons we hope to teach you in this book.

Many thanks to my daughter, Nicole Woods of Fierce Image Photography. She is responsible for the author photographs and cover art. Her photography and artistic ability are true gifts from God. Thank you for all your creative suggestions and help. I love you.

Finally, to my coauthor, Penny Dunning: None of this would be possible without you. I knew there was something special about you from the first day we met. As our friendship has grown, you have become a driving force in my focus to follow the plans God has laid out for me. You were the one to challenge me to find my passion and then pursue it. As soon as I figured out what my passion was, you were willing and eager to join me in this adventure. Your spirit continually encourages and drives me, and I look forward to each work session to see where God will lead us next.

Penny Dunning

Alone I am nothing but the dust of the earth. God, family, and friends have helped to mold and shape this book. It is amazing how God's blessings and challenges always match the task at hand. God threw down a challenge to write this book through Rick and my heart was pricked to respond. I am grateful that the Lord has blessed me with the insight, skills, and mentors in my life to be able to share what is in this book. May you be blessed in finding your soul mate and love in your lifetime.

Foreword

God leads us in some of the most unexpected directions. For Penny and me, this is one of them. One day while on the phone with her, we were discussing my desire to write a book about relationships and the premise of this book. Penny offered some great insight, and in an instant I asked her to be my co-author. And in another instant she said yes. We don't doubt for one second that God put us in this place and at this time to collaborate on this project.

This book is designed to help you find your soul mate or an extraordinary relationship. We will use these terms interchangeably throughout the book. There is a great way to find and sustain relationships, and we will help you discover that path in the following chapters. Our interest is to help you be clear about what you really want...what you are really looking for in your next relationship. We want to help you find the right relationship and weed out the inappropriate ones before you invest a significant amount of time or, worse yet, marry the wrong person. Is this book the end all and be all in finding your soul mate? Absolutely not! What we are presenting here are techniques for better self-awareness and improving your decision-making process. Through better self-awareness and decision-making ability, you start to set yourself up for a successful relationship and less heartache. Learning how to spend your time productively in your search is what we are after.

We believe that God (or whatever greater power you believe in) will guide you to the right person. When you are in the right relationship, you will "feel" or "sense" that it is correct. Some call it a "gut feeling" or intuition. Regardless of what you call it, there is an incredible sense of knowing you are with the right person.

There is a lot of information out there available to help fix relationships that are troubled, whether you are single or married. However, there seems to be very little information available to help you find or choose the right mate in the first place. We believe that if you make the right choices up front, there won't be that much to work on *after* you are in a relationship or are married. Please don't misunderstand; every relationship takes work and constant nurturing. If you are with the right person, your soul mate, the work of nurturing the relationship becomes almost effortless.

There is also a lot of information out there that will teach you "tricks" to get the man or woman of your dreams. Do you really want to trick someone into dating you? What happens when he or she finds out they have been tricked? What happens when the person of your dreams finds out you are not really who you made yourself out to be? What happens when you find out that the man or woman of your dreams was not what you really wanted? We are not going to focus on anything but dealing with basic human nature and commonsense techniques to help you in your endeavor to find your soul mate and experience a connection with someone that transcends description.

Dating Backward is the process of looking back over your past successes and mistakes in relationships, reversing the usual social expectations of dating, and becoming a hesitant lover. The foundation of dating backward is being cautious with your heart and soul while waiting for that extraordinary relationship or your soul mate.

Chapter 1

What is a soul mate?

The concept of a soul mate is foreign to many people, and it is foreign to men more so than women. Less than ten years ago, Rick would have told you there is no such thing and that it was just a loony fantasy to which women subscribe. Since then he has come to believe very strongly in the concept of soul mates and to believe that we all have the potential to have one or more in our lives. Penny always believed that soul mates existed or could be developed as a relationship grows. She has since discovered that you cannot grow or develop into a soul mate, but can discover or uncover him or her in your lifetime. We have received resistance from a few people along the way about the concept of soul mates and whether they even exist. If you don't believe in the concept of a soul mate, consider the term "extraordinary relationship." We believe the terms "soul mate" and "extraordinary relationship" can be one and the same and can be interchangeable. If you are skeptical of this kind of relationship or are in the category of nonbeliever, please keep an open mind as you read on and consider the possibility that an extraordinary relationship does exist and can be found in your lifetime. We are here to teach you how to discover and uncover that kind of relationship.

A soul mate is that person you easily connect with. This connection occurs completely on multiple levels, or the Four Relationship Cornerstones: intellectual, emotional, spiritual, and physical. These connections are more than infatuation or lust. Being with your soul mate will provide you with a sense of excitement along with a sense of calm and the feeling of completion. Communication with a soul mate is a shared understanding that is supernatural in nature in the written, spoken, and unspoken forms. Your soul mate can be the other half of what and who you are. It cannot be manufactured, changed, or purchased. To help you discover your soul mate, you need to understand yourself, the Four Relationship Cornerstones mentioned above, the love language(s) you speak, and the love language(s) that nurture your soul. In his book *The 5 Love Languages*, Gary Chapman describes the love languages as Acts of Service, Physical Touch, Gifts, Quality Time, and Words of Affirmation. He then helps you understand the primary language you speak and what language meets your soul's needs. It is our opinion that you and your soul mate will more than likely speak the same primary love language(s). While this is not an absolute, it does make communication at an extraordinary level much easier.

Communication that occurs with your soul mate across all Four Relationship Cornerstones is so strong, so great, that you can discuss virtually any subject. It is through emotional, spiritual, intellectual, and physical connections that communication and bonds are formed to make an extraordinary relationship. An extraordinary relationship with a soul mate is a two-way street of give and take between two souls with utmost consideration for each other in every possible way. Communication is the vehicle that strengthens the bonds within the Four Relationship Cornerstones. These conversations may not always be easy, but you will feel safe to have them. You both need to be emotionally and socially mature enough to listen to your mate. If you or your mate tend to retaliate with caustic, hurtful, hateful words that can never be taken back, you may have emotional or social maturity issues, which do not lead to an extraordinary relationship. Soul mates are emotionally mature. While soul mates may not have extraordinary communication styles, they are able to communicate extraordinarily well with each other. A soul mate will be *the* match for his or her mate.

Not all individuals are mature or communicate well. Assuming you, the reader, are emotionally mature and communicate effectively, you will need to be able to screen out those who are emotionally immature and have poor communication styles that conflict with your needs in a mate. With your soul mate drama and stress are naturally kept to a minimum, or within the parameters of the relationship that are comfortable for both of you. What is stressful and constitutes drama to one may not to another. It is important to understand what creates stress and drama for you and your mate and communicate these issues with each other.

A sign of a strong, mature person is that there is little or no drama, stress, or mental and physical illness in their life. Maturity brings the ability to:

- Deal with reality constructively.

- Adapt to change.

- Make long-range choices.

- Have a reasonable degree of independence.

- Have a concern for other people.

- Have a satisfactory relationship with others.

- Work productively.

In a mature relationship, individuals respect and feel joy for their mate and are able to share those special qualities and values. Soul mates are two unique individuals who connect to become stronger and more powerful as a couple. The relationship math equation is $1 + 1 = 1^{10}$. Together, you become greater, more creative, more inspirational, and more effective in life than you are individually. There is a natural synchronization of mind, body, and spirit that creates a deep, abiding love for each other.

Meanings of love

There are different types of love. The Greek language has several different words for love, while the English language has only one word with multiple meanings. In English, you can love ice cream, which is different from loving your dog, which is different from loving your children, which is different from loving your mate, which is different than the love for God. Most of the Greek versions are discussed in the Bible. Here are the four most common types of love in no particular order.

- *Storge* means affection in ancient and modern Greek. It is natural affection, like that felt by parents for children. The word is used almost exclusively as a descriptor of relationships with the family. A common example in the American culture today is "motherly love." This is one of the stronger loves because it involves a commitment that relies only on one characteristic of the receiver of the love, and that is that he or she is a dependent.

- *Philos*, or *phileo*, means friendship or affectionate love in modern Greek. It is a dispassionate, virtuous love, a concept developed by Aristotle. It includes loyalty to friends, family, and community and requires virtue, equality, and familiarity. In ancient texts, *philos* denoted a general type of love, used for love between family, friends, or lovers, as well as a desire for or enjoyment of an activity. When Jesus wept following the death of His dear friend Lazarus, the onlookers remarked, "See how he loved (*phileo*) him!" (John 11:36). Another example would be "After David had finished talking with Saul, Jonathan became one in spirit with David, and he loved him as himself" (1 Samuel 18:1). In an extraordinary relationship, *philos* will be present because your soul mate will be your best friend.

- *Eros* is the root word for "erotic" but does not describe sexual love only. It actually describes all emotional love...the feeling of love. As an emotion, it is morally neutral. It can lead just as easily to lust as it can to passion. It can be a passionate love with sensual desire and longing, which is how we most commonly think of *eros*. *Eros* can be interpreted as a love for someone whom you love with more than *philia*, the love of friendship. It can also apply to dating relationships as well as marriage. *Eros* within a dating relationship is designed to be morally pure and without passionate lust. *Eros* within marriage is designed by God for physical and emotional pleasure. You can have passion for a person without passionate lust, aware that physical purity is necessary for spiritual purity. You will experience *eros* with your soul mate, hopefully with passion while dating, and save the physical pleasure for your mate until after you are married. We will discuss physical intimacy in chapter 7 of this book.

- *Agape* is unselfish love, unconditional love...a commitment to seek the best and highest good for another person, regardless of any response. In the ancient Greek, it often refers to a general affection or deeper sense of "true love" rather than the attraction suggested by *eros*. Agape love is not in any way dependent on circumstances, because it says "I love you because I choose to." This kind of love for your mate will be one without expectations, no strings attached, and you will love expecting nothing in return. Your love will be all about him or her...all about your soul mate.

Why is it important to know what the different types of love are? You have to understand the different types or qualities of love to make sure you understand what you are feeling and what you are looking for. It helps you distinguish between infatuation and being in a loving relationship. The ultimate love in an extraordinary relationship is *agape* love. This is unconditional love. When you are in an extraordinary relationship and have unconditional love, you are with your soul mate! In this relationship you will experience *philos* and *eros* also, but they will be surrounded or wrapped in *agape* love. In an online article titled "Love and Dating: How Most Singles Have Love Backwards, June Hunt states

Most dating starts with *eros*. In fact, many couples never move beyond this phase. Those who do move past "romantic" love typically move to *phileo*, the affectionate love of genuinely liking. This route, however, rarely leads to *agape*—unconditional love that seeks what is in the best interest of the other person—because it's hijacked along the way by selfishness, lust, or any number of other relational roadblocks.

Unconditional love without expectations is not easy to find. The key is patience. Other than with God, you will not find *agape* love just anywhere. It is out there and you will need to be discerning about the relationship that you enter into. Once you have experienced *agape* love, you will never want to settle for any other type of all-encompassing love in a relationship. Knowing that your significant other is so totally in love with you and you totally in love with her or him is the ultimate in relationships. There is a freedom to love and be loved for who you are and without demands or expectations. This should be the goal of everyone looking for a substantial long-term relationship. Without this type of love, at best you will have a great relationship. It will never be extraordinary.

Relationships that are not soul mate quality

Relationships that are less than extraordinary are often filled with drama. Most causes of drama are related to emotional immaturity. These individuals are often known as drama queens (or kings) who can suck the life out of a relationship. They are self-centered narcissistic people who are emotionally unavailable for anyone but themselves. Stress and drama can be self-created through communications, actions, and the daily choices they make. This negative tension is the driving force for this individual and often takes energy from all positive people, values, and social settings around them. When you come across someone like this, red flags should pop up. Politely excuse yourself from the conversation and leave the room. Don't worry; there will be plenty of others to take your place in their life, and it will free you from excess drama and open the door for you to find your soul mate.

In college, Penny dated a young man, and initially there were good times, communication, and laughter together. Penny said, "It was an instant connection, or so I thought. Looking back, I really missed the red flags of his emotional immaturity and should have terminated the relationship early on." Over the three months of dating, I began to notice changes in his behavior and our relationship. He demanded my full attention and became jealous at parties when I socialized with other friends. If he failed to get the attention he demanded, he would begin to pout and close down communication and withdraw his kindness. His remarks would become snide and cutting. The negative communication, control and acting out were unrecognized red flags and he lacked emotional maturity. His increased expectations were unreasonable. Emotionally mature people do not cut down, belittle, or speak words of harm in an effort to make themselves appear more intelligent, funny, or the life of a party at someone else's expense. He would say, "It was just a joke, quit being so sensitive." At this point I should have recognized this kind of communication as disrespectful and harmful and walked away. Rick and I will discuss the harmful effects that this type of emotionally immature relationship can have on a person in chapter 3.

"It was not long after that when I missed another red flag. Issues of control were growing and became problematic. He was moody if I spent time with my girlfriends, went shopping, or had lunch out.", stated Penny. My time was not my own, and there was a lack of respect growing between us. There was a beginning feeling that I could not plan any activities or have enjoyment outside of our relationship or without his approval. There was a loss of self-choice, self-direction, and friendships. Friends are life's treasures, and we are blessed to have them in our lives. A true love or soul mate will respect your values, time, and friends. If by chance your friends are poor choices, a mature and true love will openly communicate by speaking to you kindly, with concern and love in his or her heart for your well-being.

Emotionally immature individuals disrespect your time, values, and choices that do not revolve around them, and they can ultimately seek to control you.

One evening Penny discovered that, "Owning your contributions to a failed relationship is the first step to obtain a mature relationship." My boyfriend shared the problems that he had in his first marriage with his ex-wife. It was awful to hear that his ex-wife became so angry with him that she took a claw hammer and beat him with it. I wondered, "What on earth would make a woman so mad that she felt the need to beat another human being with a claw hammer?" According to him, it was all her fault and he had done nothing to provoke that fit of anger. It was at this time that instincts or gut feelings took over and told me something was not right. It was at this point where clarity and courage to end the relationship happened. My personal goals and values did not match his. I knew that this was not the kind of person I wanted to marry. He lacked the values of respect, integrity, honesty, and maturity. I knew it was best to end the relationship. He planned on leaving the state without me, but before he left there were two more times when he came to the house and stood outside ringing the doorbell and waited in the driveway. It was a bit stressful feeling and it was like hiding out in my own home. The truth was, there was no desire to answer the door, and I was finished with the relationship. I knew that owning my responsibility to a failure was necessary to be successful.

Please note that this is a very important teaching moment in ending relationships. Do not open the door, accept phone calls, e-mails, texts, or letters, or allow any other type of communication. If you do, you allow that person to enter back into your life to try to control you all over again. Done is done, over is over, and when you end this type of relationship, it is time to move on to the future. It was a great relief when he finally moved out of state. This experience was life changing for me (Penny) and created a feeling of fear and left me a bit unsure of my judgment in men. If only I had been taught about emotional immaturity, what it looked like, and that it is best to end relationships like this very early on. You cannot fix the emotionally immature individual. You did not break them, and you cannot fix them. The best option is recognizing this and moving on.

Foundation for a mature, successful relationship

Emotional maturity begins with an honest evaluation of your personal values, your response to life situations, and your relationships. Where you grew up, who raised you, the era in which you were born, your economic status, school experiences, your religious upbringing, and everything else, positive and negative, that has happened to you in your life will influence your value system. What is said, what is not said, what is done, and what is not done all express values. A core value system that does not change is a sign of a healthy, mature person. Your soul mate and you gain energy and grow from your experiences as individuals and as a couple. You admire, respect, and love each other.

As human beings, when we are young, we tend to be wide eyed and naïve about relationships and have poor insight to our values. We are overwhelmed with infatuation and lack the experience and understanding about life and the Four Relationship Cornerstones that make relationships successful. We tend to follow society's pre-scription for dating, infatuation, being head over heels, and crazy in love. What is valued in relationships during our teens and twenties is very different from what is important to us at forty or fifty years of age and beyond. Living life is guaranteed to change your list of things that are important, and it will continue to evolve as you travel through life. Dating backward is the ability to look at an individual and yourself before going forward into a relationship. Extraordinary relationships grow and evolve through life in tandem together. While you may not grow in the same areas or in the same direction, you will share in the joy of your mate's growth. Relationships that are not successful or extraordinary tend to experience change that is not communicated or shared as a life experience. Growth as individuals and as a couple is often lacking or missing in relationships that fail.

Infatuation is an incredible aphrodisiac and deludes the inexperienced into thinking it is true love. It is so powerful that we overlook serious flaws in the people we date, court, and even marry. As described in his book *The 5 Love Languages*, Gary Chapman explains the effect of infatuation or "the obsessive stage of love" on relationships. It has been observed that infatuation will last, on average, for two years. When we make decisions based on infatuation, we are often totally incorrect and will probably regret our decisions later on down the road. Infatuation does not mean you are with your soul mate. It may be an indication of *eros* love but not true or *agape* love, which you should be looking for. A true soul mate is able to demonstrate *agape* love across the Four Relationship Cornerstones with extraordinary communication.

When you are infatuated with someone, you may see the imperfections in them that you are not willing to live with long-term but you gloss over them. You may ignore the imperfections, you may think you can change the imperfections in your mate or believe that the imperfection will somehow magically disappear. Infatuation causes chemical changes in the brain similar to narcotics and is very addictive. There are those who cannot continue relationships because of the lack of the infatuation feeling and because they need to feel it over and over again. They are "forever daters" and can never commit to a long-term relationship. The chemical change can cloud perception and judgment in the same way narcotics can. Under the influences of these chemical changes, it is easy to gloss over unhealthy relationship characteristics and make errors in judgment. The impact of these chemical changes and self-talk allows us to draw conclusions that may take years to understand before we discover they are erroneous. The singular belief that "He or she will change in time and come to a greater understanding like mine" is a relationship death trap. And often, several years into a relationship or marriage, we realize that the change didn't happen no matter what we said or tried to do to "help" them change. Change can only come from within, not from outside pressure. In spite of any encouragement (which usually turns to nagging and cajoling in unhealthy relationships), your mate can change themselves only if they desire to make the change. Some of us, even as we age, never learn this lesson and are doomed to repeat this error again and again. Infatuation blinds us to the realities of the relationship (or the lack of one). This is why it is so very important to understand how infatuation affects us and to always look realistically at a new relationship. If there are aspects of his or her character that you cannot live with for the rest of your life, it is time to end the relationship before it goes any further, because these character traits will not change.

Do you know and love yourself?

You must know yourself and love yourself before you can know or love another. You must understand what you like and what you don't like. You have to know what excites you, what gives you the desire to get out of bed in the morning, and where your passion lies. Just stop reading for a moment and think about this concept. Start writing in your journal all the things that you enjoy in life. This exercise can accomplish a couple of different things. First, it will help you decide what makes you happy, excited, and motivated. Second, it will help you to start defining some of the things you might be looking for in a mate.

The characteristics of your mate are very important, but for now, let's focus on you. Does a good book excite you? What about attending sporting events? How about lying on a beach? Does something at work excite you and motivate you? How about acquiring a new client or creating an award-winning presentation? Do you love photography or painting? Are you great with your hands—maybe a mechanic, a carpenter, a cake decorator? If you are drawing a blank and you are just not coming up with anything, ask yourself: "What could I be excited about?" Start building your list from there. You don't have to have a long list of things you are excited about. It might be just a couple of things. The more you think about it, the more you are likely to see your list grow.

An example of what we are talking about here is that one day Penny and I were discussing work, and I expressed some displeasure with my chosen career at the time. Penny paused and asked me something that no one had ever asked before. She asked, "What are you passionate about?" At that moment in time I didn't know. There are a lot of things that bring enjoyment, however, they are not things that would get me to jump out of bed in the morning and hit the floor running. With some soul searching, some prayer, and some quiet time, I realized God had placed writing this book on my heart. This subject is my passion and fascination. It is also about helping people...helping them start to think and helping guide them in the right direction. It is about presenting some commonsense information about relationships that most people just never think of. If you are struggling with coming up with things that excite you, take some time to be quiet and just let your mind wander. This is a great time to just reflect on what is important to you and what motivates you.

Why do you need to love yourself? It may sound a bit self-centered, but if you don't or can't love yourself, who will? Pick up a mirror and look deeply into it. Who or what do you see looking back? Beauty is in the eye of the beholder, and what you see in yourself is projected for others to observe. When people don't love themselves, they believe it is because of some inherent flaws. A universal truth is that if you do not love yourself, you prevent yourself from being loved by anyone else. This can be corrected with a re-evaluation of your self-perception. You need to be comfortable and confident with yourself as you are. By loving yourself, you are accepting yourself for who you are. If you don't love and don't like yourself, you will not be able to fully love others. We all have traits that can be improved on, and we all have traits that are unique, making us precious, lovable, and beautiful. How can you expect someone to love you when you view the person you see in the mirror as inadequate? Others will sense this too and will not be willing to get involved with you in any kind of deep, meaningful, healthy relationship. There is not one person alive who wants to spend his or her waking hours working toward pleasing or convincing someone of his or her worth and value. It is also a great thing when you share positive feedback with someone you love, but having to reinforce this daily drains you of precious energy. A soul mate will not drain you and leave you feeling empty. They will meet you where you are, love you for who you are, and accept whatever weaknesses you may have. Loving others fully and completely is the basis of an extraordinary relationship because you will not be holding anything back.

Define the relationship you desire

In this section, we want to start off by helping you define your expectations for a relationship. Let's take a look at the type of relationship you want. There are a couple of questions that come to mind when we think about relationships. Are you looking for a long-term relationship, something that could lead to marriage? Or are you looking for a short-term, casual relationship, just a friend to do things with on the weekends or an evening during the week and nothing serious? Before you start your search, you need to start with an idea of where you want your relationship to go.

Set the expectations early so, first and foremost, *you* know what you want and, secondly, so that your prospective mate knows what you are looking for. While this may seem pretty basic, it is amazing how many people just start looking and have only a vague idea—no specifics of the relationship they are looking for. Having a vague idea about the type of relationship you want is akin to setting out on a road trip without a map. You may have a general heading but are unlikely to reach your destination because you don't have any specific direction.

Determine the personal characteristics you are looking for

Our emotions create desires, goals, and life dreams to bring us a sense of accomplishment and joy. Dreams are created for the things we most desire in life. What is your heart's desire for a mate? Are you dreaming of a relationship that is intensely intimate, without walls, where you are so connected that you think and act as one? Are you dreaming of a man or woman who honors your intelligence and allows you the freedom to be you? Is your dream of two happy, separate individuals that are so connected that their responses and actions are as if they are one person? Have you ever dreamed of being so close to someone you can feel their joy and pain without speaking to them? We want you to seek your dreams and make them a reality, and to know what to do when reality is not matching your dreams.

What characteristics are you looking for in a relationship? What is your ideal mate like? These are two key questions we need to review next. Beginning your search starts with a sheet of paper with one side titled "My Soul Mate" and the other side "Me." Each side will have two columns: one of them with the heading "Positive" and the other "Negative." This list will be a work in progress and one you will revise and update as you grow and become clearer on who you are and what you want and need in a relationship. An example is provided below.

My Soul Mate	
Must Have List or Positive	Deal Breaker List or Negative
Emotional	Emotional
Intellectual	Intellectual
Spiritual	Spiritual
Physical	Physical
Communication	Communication
What I am looking for:	Deal Breakers:

My Self-evaluation	
Must Have List or Positive	Deal Breaker List or Negative
Emotional	Emotional
Intellectual	Intellectual
Spiritual	Spiritual
Physical	Physical
Communication	Communication
What I am looking for:	Deal Breakers:

On your sheet of paper or in your journal, start to make notes about your ideal relationship. List the relationship characteristics you want in the positive column. These need to be *your* wants and not what anyone else thinks you should be looking for. The idea is to define what is important to you—what *you* must have and also what the Deal Breakers are. The Deal Breakers will go in the negative column. There will be certain minor things or characteristics that may be acceptable if that person possesses virtually all of your Must Haves. You should never settle for anyone that has any characteristics that you would normally consider Deal Breakers.

Continue to develop your list of Must Haves in the positive column to describe the person you are looking for. Include physical characteristics—tall, short, blond, brunet, fit, about average, curvy, long hair, short hair, blue eyes, hazel eyes, etc. Be as specific as you can. Some people aren't as interested in looks as others. If looks are not as important, then your list may not be as detailed. Men are generally more visual, so guys, your list will probably be longer. Women, on the other hand, tend to see more of the person on the inside, so ladies, your lists may be a little vaguer when it comes to looks, but longer with personality traits, characteristics, and needs. Note: the more Must Haves you have, the narrower the field of possibilities will be.

Personality is important. Do you want someone who is quiet, someone who can be the life of the party, or someone in between? Should he or she be very open and direct, or do you find a more reserved and quiet personality to be attractive?

What other characteristics are important to you? What about income? Is a clean house important? Do you have or want pets? Do you have or want children? Is faith important to you? What about politics? What are your personal goals, and is it important to have someone that shares your dreams and goals with you? Are you open to new experiences or do you like routine? Do you want private "me" time or do you want to spend all of your free time together? Is personal hygiene important to you? What about saving and spending money? These are just a few of the characteristics that should be considered. Virtually anything that you consider important in a relationship should be added to your list. Always state your preferences in the positive. Framing your Must Haves in the positive helps keep you from looking at potential relationships with negative thoughts. For example, if you want someone that is active, rather than saying "No couch potatoes," say something like "Must be active or adventurous." Here are some examples of writing positive Must Haves.

- Must be willing to help clean the house.

- Must want to be with me but not need me.

- Must be a Christian with strong morals and values.

- Must earn a respectable living.

- Must be politically conservative/liberal.

- Must have a strong personality.

- Must have personal goals.

- Must enjoy modest personal displays of affection.

- Must have a positive attitude.

- Must be able to communicate effectively.

- Must be intelligent, not necessarily educated.

- Must be healthy physically and emotionally.

If you are serious about seeking a soul mate, these are all things that you need to be thinking about, adding to your list, and refining your list as you date. Some people you meet will automatically be dropped as a potential mate even before the first date. Some will be eliminated after a couple of e-mails or phone calls. A few will make it to a first date, and it will be "one and done." A select few will make it past the first week, maybe a month or longer. If you pay attention to what you listed as important characteristics, you will be able to very quickly eliminate anyone who does not meet your criteria.

Rick was having a phone conversation with a woman that he had met. In one of their previous conversations, the subject of politics came up (because that subject is important to him). They discovered that they didn't necessarily agree on the topic. Rick is very decisive and opinionated, and she was, for lack of better terms, wishy washy and very unsure of what to believe. She took offense to Rick's position and the importance that he placed on the topic. She commented that she didn't believe that we needed to have a cookie-cutter mate to have a great relationship. She believed that you didn't necessarily have to be on the same page to be able to get along. For her, that may be true. For Rick, it is not. Experience tells us that the more things two people have in common, the stronger their relationship will be, because they will have less to disagree about. The more disagreements or arguments you can remove from a relationship up front, the fewer arguments you are going to have down the road. If you are not on the same page about the big things—the things that are most important to you—you cannot develop a deep connection on all levels. We believe that you cannot develop a deep, spiritual connection with someone who doesn't have the same fundamental beliefs in God that you do. The same holds true for the intellectual, emotional, and physical aspects of a relationship.

Is it important that someone meet every characteristic on your list? That is up to you. Are you willing to settle for less than extraordinary? If not, then you need to keep looking for the one with all the characteristics you are searching for. The more specific you are, the more likely you are to find your soul mate, but it may take you a longer period of time to find exactly what you are looking for. There are a number of other factors that need to be in place for this person to be your soul mate, but this is a good start for now. We will discuss these other factors in later chapters.

One of the things Rick experienced in finding his first soul mate is that while a man may continue to see beauty in other women, we tend to start comparing them to what we already have and quickly realize that there is no real comparison. When you are with your soul mate, you instinctively know that you already have the very best in your mate and there is no one else who can compare. This is a fundamental principle of extraordinary relationships. You realize and understand that there is no reason to look any further because the person you are with is the one that makes you complete. There will always be a more physically attractive person out there, but none that has all the unique qualities of your soul mate that attracted you in the first place. This is absolutely the most incredible feeling that one can have. It is so deep and absolute that there is no question in either of your minds as to who is the most important person in your life. This is the chemistry that people talk about. It is that connection that allows you to look across the room and smile just because you know he or she is with you. And, if you doubt this, strike up a conversation with the most beautiful person (man or woman) you can find. You will soon see that there are significant interpersonal qualities that are missing for them to be a great match for you. You will not connect with him or her because some part of the equation is missing—the spiritual, intellectual, or emotional connection will not be there. Looks alone are never the sole characteristic that will make an extraordinary mate.

Penny and Rick have both independently come to know the power of identifying high-priority characteristics that they desire in their individual extraordinary relationships. The more specific you are in defining your ideal mate, the better your chances of finding that person are. Time is finite. We are given only so much of it on this earth. Wasting time on bad dates is not beneficial to anyone; not you and not your date. By being patient and taking time to screen your prospective dates and make sure they meet most of your criteria up front, you will eliminate a lot of unnecessary dates and some of the painfully uncomfortable situations you would otherwise find yourself in. Weeding out incompatible candidates is not a judgment that a person is bad; it just means that he or she is not right for you. Dating is work, and even with the best screening efforts you will find that there are those "one and done" dates, or after several dates the true character of the individual surfaces and you must end the relationship because of the game playing or deception that was experienced.

It is our belief that there is no one right answer to any of the questions that follow. There are as many answers as there are people answering the questions. And there are countless more questions you can ask. Here are some examples of questions you can ask yourself about the characteristics you are looking for in a mate:

- Do I want to have someone to travel with?

- Do I like adventure?

- Am I a homebody who likes to do things around the yard?

- Am I social and do I like to entertain, or do I like to have quiet meals at home?

- Is religion important to me?

- What about personality? Do I want someone with a strong personality or someone who is laid back?

These are just a few questions to get you started. The sky is the limit as far as the number of questions you can ask yourself. The more detailed your list, the more specific you can be about your ideal relationship.

As you start to define the relationship you are looking for and start to create the picture in your mind, don't think that this list is carved in stone. Don't be afraid to make adjustments to what you find important to your ideal relationship. As you date, you will have experiences that may or may not be good, and they will help you refine your list of Must Haves. Defining what you want is the basis for setting any goal. Finding your soul mate is no different. As you work on your list mentioned above, write all those positive things you desire in your mate, such as physical appearance, emotional expressions, intelligence, and spirituality. These positive traits give you a measuring rod for your potential mate. In the Deal Breaker or negative list, include all those things that you are not willing to live with and that are undesirable characteristics in your mate. Keep this list in a safe place because you will use it over and over. From time to time you will modify this list and update it as you mature and grow. Many things make impressions on us in our life. We need to evaluate these impressions, determine whether they are positive or negative, and utilize that information to help make better choices.

What do you bring to the relationship?

Next, let's take a look at what you bring to a potential relationship. What are your characteristics that make you attractive to someone else? Are you caring and nurturing? Are you bold and outgoing? Do you have a positive or negative attitude? In other words, is your glass half full or half empty? Or does your cup runneth over? What skills or talents do you have? Ask some of your closest friends or family to help you answer these questions. You need to make sure they give you *honest* feedback. Be prepared to learn positive things about yourself and things that you may need to change.

What are some of the things you need to improve on? Do you have a temper? Do you have low self-esteem? What characteristics do you have that a potential mate might find unattractive? For example, Rick had a conversation with a woman about her relationship with her current boyfriend. She had indoor cats. Her boyfriend was raised on a farm and didn't believe that animals belonged in the house, and he complained that there was cat hair in the house. She insisted that she didn't want to get rid of the cats *and* was not motivated to do the extra cleaning necessary to be able to keep her boyfriend happy. This created a huge roadblock in their relationship. Rick's suggestion was that she make the extra effort to clean up the cat hair each week, get rid of the cats, or leave the relationship. As long as she remains un-motivated to do a little more (in this case extra cleaning), she is telegraphing to her boyfriend that he is not worth the extra effort in her mind. What do you think the odds of this relationship lasting are? Our belief is that if you are in an ideal or extraordinary relationship, the extra effort would seem effortless because of the value you place on your mate's desires and needs. This is not to say that you have to jump through hoops to please someone with a domineering personality.

Often our ideals of what a perfect mate would be are formed from what we see in our parents, grandparents, family, friends, and even the movies we watch. You form a picture in your mind and heart as to what the perfect mate and relationship will look like. You see things you like and dislike in relationships around you and create your own version of extraordinary. Review your thoughts and ideas and evaluate them to see if they will help you create and refine your lists.

What a soul mate looks like to the world

Movies are rich with story lines where men and women are perfect in their response to each other with a commitment of their undying love and will go to any length to demonstrate that love to each other. The popular movie series *Twilight* is based on the young female, Bella, who is attracted to Edward. She has a need for love and belonging, and Edward has been searching over one hundred years for the love of his life. As the story unfolds, both Bella and Edward fall hopelessly, eternally in love and discover they are soul mates. The love they share is shown as one that is extraordinary. Either will go to the ends of the earth to protect, love, and be connected to the other. There is a short period of confusion and challenge for Bella when Jacob expresses his love for her, but for Bella, no one but Edward will do. Jacob is confused, thinking that he alone can give Bella everything she needs and is better for her than Edward. Bella chooses Edward and his lifestyle because it is closest to her spirit, intellect, and emotional makeup. There are many more movies, novels, and life stories that provide example after example of these connections to create an extraordinary love based on the authors' ideals. The problem that results in reality is that people will base their relationship desires on something they have seen in the movies or what they have witnessed in someone else's relationship, and their love goal is to seek and re-create that story in their life. We all have our own unique story of love that we need to discover. We cannot live and love in a fantasy world or according to another person's ideals. This is an important concept to understand. You must focus on what *you* want in a relationship. It makes no difference what others think is right for you. Only you (and God) know what is really in your heart and what you truly desire. You may be mocked or scoffed at, but in the end, this is *your* soul mate you are looking for...no one else's.

Real life most often presents a different picture from the movies or our dreams. Somehow it is never as quick, smooth, or easy as the story in the book, on the screen, or during our dream state. Real life is complicated with our fears, hurts, desires, and emotions. The environment and genetics you were raised with cannot be changed. The thing you can do is alter your reality or how you look at life. To make your dreams and desires come true, you need to adjust your perception of the environment you were raised in and how you learned as a child to cope with life. Look at your reality objectively, and you will see that even the negative things in your life can have a positive side. In seeking your extraordinary relationship, you will encounter relationships that cause both joy and pain. It is through these experiences that you learn and craft your list of Must Haves and Deal Breakers. The broken road of your life is what is leading you into your dreams and living out your happiness. It is well worth the time to wait for and seek out your soul mate.

It is easy to model our desires and search out the story lines of a movie, book, or dream. The problem is that it is not your own personal story. Choices that lead to failures and relationships that do not last occur because the choice is made prematurely, reality is not taken into account, or there is a willingness to settle for less than extraordinary in a mate. Have you ever thought, "I will help them understand and he or she will change." Or have you felt the connection of a sexual attraction for which you are willing to sacrifice your intellectual, emotional, and spiritual connections? Delusion is a common way to cope in real life and blinds us from reality. Remember, you can change your perception of the environment you were raised in, and only you can change your ability to cope. Seeing the denial of your coping pattern will help you to see the reality of the relationship and its true potential in your life.

Beginning your soul mate search through dating

Dating is the modern-day vehicle that we use to look for the ideal mate. In times past, relationships were prearranged for financial or political gain. In our modern culture we are given the opportunity to choose our mate. Time is spent getting to know someone better to determine how close they come to being our ideal mate. Have you ever been in a store shopping and you have an intense surge of energy pulse through you? You turn around and find your eyes locking with someone else's, and there is that instant connection. You are total strangers, and yet there is something electrical, palpable, and very real that exists in that moment. You think, "This must be the one!" One glance at their hand and you see that they are married. How can it be so right and yet so wrong? Real life throws us curve balls. That is part of life.

Dating opportunities can be found online through various dating or connection services, work, school, church, civic groups, or other social activities. People should take great care to seek out opportunities to find that extraordinary connection with that spark, that very palpable electricity from *the one*. Hours can be spent searching, going through e-mails, reading dating site profiles, and searching for those who begin to fulfill your personal Must Have list. Introductions can come from friends; you can be led by a higher being or purely by chance. Before you date you need to look at your personal desires and needs in a relationship. This is foundational to success in finding an extraordinary relationship and finding that ideal mate.

Reasonable measures should be taken to obtain the desired time with someone in an effort to validate or negate the possibility of the ideal mate. The more time you are able to spend with a person, the more you will get to know them in their environment as well as your own. It is important to get to know your potential mate in both your environment and theirs because the true person comes out. We all tend to be on our best behavior for the first few dates, or maybe even as much as the first few months.

As time and your budding relationship progress, the walls or the facades start to come down. As they do, the real personalities of you and your partner start to emerge. This is when the real in-depth evaluation of your relationship can begin. This is also the time when you will need to be brutally honest with yourself and your mate. Assuming all aspects of your relationship have been good so far, this is when red flags or problems will start to show up. As these concerns arise, open, healthy conversations are in order to determine if these are going to be major or minor problems. Are they a matter of super-ficial personal habits that can easily and willingly be addressed, or are they deep character issues that are deal breakers or even more serious issues that may need professional help? The idea in this dis-covery phase is not necessarily to try to change your partner to fit your needs and desires, but to discover whether you are a good fit for each other. What we think you will find is that minor issues will be easily remedied if you are with the right person. If you are with the wrong person, minor issues will never go away and will only grow in magnitude as your relationship progresses.

You have to maintain your resolve and be true to yourself in your search for your soul mate. Many well-intentioned people will ques-tion your methods and your goals. People will say it is unrealistic to have such a narrow focus on what you are looking for in a rela-tionship. They will tell you that you need to be open to unexpected opportunities and to be flexible about your list. People who want to date you will question your decision and try to convince you that you are wrong and that they are a great match for you. The purpose of making a list of personal and relationship characteristics is to help you define what *you* want and what is right for you. It is to give you focus and clarity about what is needed to help keep you on track during your search. Refer to your list regularly until you have it memorized. This is an important step because it will help you from becoming side-tracked by someone who has some great qualities but not all of the qualities you are looking for in an extraordinary relationship. The characteristics of your soul mate have to be based on your wants, needs, and desires and no one else's. As we said earlier, you can continue to refine your list as you date and discover other characteristics that are important to you or traits that are deal breakers. Only you know what is right for you. It is up to you not to settle for anything less than extraordinary.

Chapter 2

Life's journey and the baggage we collect

The soul mate search is a journey and can begin at any stage or phase of life. It takes wisdom to search for and find that special person at any stage of life, but more so when you have never been married. The relationship stages of being single, divorced, or widowed will bring unique challenges to your search for a soul mate. Each and every stage of life will bring its life issues and experiences that will impact the success or limitation of your search. As we grow and move through life, we bring with us our life experiences, which we sometimes call baggage. Baggage can be defined in a number of different ways. In essence, it is the emotional stuff we carry around from our childhood, past relationships, and general life experiences. Some examples might be parent or family issues, work issues, spiritual issues, divorce, death, health, and any number of other things that you can think of. These issues will be different for everyone. Everyone comes with baggage. If people tell you differently, they are in denial. The question is, what have you packed in your bags? And what do you choose to carry around with you? Inside our bags we pack both positive and negative attitudes and experiences. On any given day, you may unpack something positive or negative. In reality, baggage is what makes us who we are today. It is what makes each of us unique. The difference is how we deal with what we have packed.

You can choose to handle your issues positively or negatively. If you are too positive, you can have a Pollyanna approach to life that may not be realistic. You could also choose to be negative, in which case nothing in the world is right. That is not necessarily the healthiest attitude to take either. A healthy approach includes a realistic view of life and is balanced somewhere in between all negative and all positive. We suggest that you tend to lean more to the positive side of life. Just a little negative can go a long way. A balanced approach to your outlook on life will be much more likely to lead to a generally happy outlook.

Happiness has to start or come from within and stems from your personal relationship with your Creator and who you are. Happiness is internal, not external. Belongings and material possessions alone have never made anyone happy. Joy starts internally and flows outward from you to others when you assume accountability and responsibility for your choices, actions, and decisions. We have found that when you sacrifice your selfishness, it is the beginning of the walk toward selflessness and true happiness. We have both experienced the loss of everything. The times when we found we had nothing are the times we found our everything in life. You are a beautiful creation and have so much good to offer. When you accept the positives and negatives within yourself, you can love yourself, and that makes room for you to love another.

Singles

We all start out as single people. Being single and looking for your soul mate requires the maturity, wisdom, and ability to delay gratification and wait on the best for you. You have to know how to search out your own heart, desires, and needs in a soul mate and be willing to wait. This is where most of us drop the ball. We live in a world of immediate gratification. In our younger formative years, we are not taught the art of waiting and being patient. This is a critical trait in being able to find your soul mate. Your patience, your ability to postpone immediate gratification, is key to making wise decisions in all aspects of your life, not just with finding an extraordinary relationship.

Your parents' marriage and your family structure can significantly impact how you look at relationships and life. They may not always be the best examples you can follow if there were problems in your parents' relationship and in your family. Initially you may have to do some work to get rid of the relationship garbage that you learned early in life. Unfortunately many marriages end in divorce because people enter into relationships out of societal expectations, guilt, impatience, willingness to settle for less than God's best, physical attraction alone, or anything else in a long list of incomplete thinking. If you are single (never been married before) and take this book seriously, you will weigh all the information and wait until you find the one who meets your needs and fulfills an extraordinary relationship for you. This can happen quickly or may take years as you grow, learn, and craft your list of what you bring to a relationship and what you desire.

Do you love your life? If you don't, how will you love life with someone else? Seek to know yourself and what brings you pleasure. Make a list of the things that bring you joy and happiness. Use this knowledge to craft your list of Must Haves. Give yourself permission to be happy and seek your personal happiness. There are many self-help books to accomplish this. Being quiet, looking inward, and feeling peace and joy are a start to understanding yourself. To find that soul mate, you have to know who you are, and then you will be able know what you want in a mate. Seek to become the happiest and very best you can be as a single person, and you will begin to draw in what you are seeking. It is a natural law of attraction. We all have things we work on or need to change, and you need to love that side of yourself too. Change is part of life, and engaging in it allows you to continue to grow and become the very best for you and your mate.

Divorce

One of the important lessons we have both learned is that there is an emotional healing and a growing process after your divorce is final. The longer you have been with someone, the longer it will take to heal. During the course of your marriage there were generally some, perhaps many, good times. It isn't until communication breaks down that the good times aren't so good anymore. At some point in time the relationship dies and there is a point of no return. Most if not all of the connections with your spouse are broken. Healing your brokenness is necessary before you embark on a search for your soul mate. This healing process really doesn't start until the divorce is final. No matter how long you have been separated, there is still healing and growth that will occur. If you have been separated for several months to even a few years, many of the negative emotions will have subsided and you will have moved on from them. However, there is something about the finality of the divorce that needs to be dealt with internally before you are ready to date again.

There will probably be a decompression time when you are just happy to be alone with your thoughts, or a strong desire to run and play and do things that you were unable to do in your previous marriage. Every individual will deal with the stress and grieve the loss of the relationship a little differently. What is common to all is that there is a period of adjustment. It could be putting the finishing touches on a new home or redecorating your existing home now that you are not married, or having new hobbies and activities. This decompression time can be as short as a few days to a year or more, depending on how adversarial your divorce was or how happy you are that it is final. When the decompression stage and adjustment are over, the real healing and growing can start to begin.

Don't be surprised if healing and growth take a year or more. In fact, growth and change are lifelong processes. With a divorce comes a huge change. Most often change is a slow process that just takes time. Rick stated, "It was a process of thirteen months before I felt like a new man. I was having a conversation with my best friend, and I was very upbeat and positive. My friend told me that he hadn't heard me sound this good in a long, long time. And he was right. I was feeling better about myself, about my life, and about the direction I was heading. Was I out of the woods? Not yet. As time passes, I find that I am still growing. I believe that most of the emotional healing is complete, but, admittedly, there are still times that I have moments of unwanted emotions."

We have had many conversations with people about the healing and growing they will do once their divorce is final. For some there is a denial for the need of healing. I (Rick) denied it too! In follow-up conversations, each person has come back and said: "You were right. I never realized the stress I was under. I thought that I was through with all of my emotions relating to my divorce." We can deny the stress; we may not even recognize it at the time. However, give yourself at least six months after your divorce to come to understand and appreciate the decompression or release of some stress, new emotions, and new freedom. This can almost be considered a time of rebirth, and time must be spent in re-evaluating what is important, what is not important, and where you want to go in life. Don't deny it; don't avoid it; revel in it and enjoy the time getting to renew and getting reacquainted with yourself.

For me, (Penny) it took two years before there was a feeling of being ready to date again. My friends recognized how stuck I was. Through their encouragement and support, they set up blind dates that helped ease breaking into the world of dating. Dating had changed so much from thirty-two years ago, I found that after divorce, the biggest question that had to be asked was what kind of relationship do I want? Was I ready for a relationship again? Many men could be looking for a mother to raise their family, others for a companion, some wanted one-night stands, and still others were looking for that "soul mate with the spark." Looking at my fears helped to identify what I was most afraid of and deal with the negative thoughts associated with dating. Addressing the societal changes in values and the dangers associated with dating seemed huge to me. The realization that not all people who are dating are homicidal sociopaths and that there are still good people in the world who do not need to be feared. I learned how to date safely and both Rick and I will share these dating suggestions with you.

Dating begins with good intentions and being very clear with the person you are dating. Being honest with that individual avoids defrauding them. Make it clear before your first date if you are searching for short-term relationships or if you are interested in seeking out long-term relationships. You should never expect a short-term relationship to transition to a long-term relationship. Being honest with yourself and with others is the basis of common courtesy and respect. All individuals deserve that courtesy and respect. When you start dating, do not do any serious dating in the first year after your divorce. It is easy to have one date and be done. This is where the dating sites and online services are helpful. They allow you an opportunity to screen individuals and talk with them prior to going on a date. You can quickly tell if there are common interests. We suggest you take your time sharing e-mails or phone calls prior to meeting someone in person. You need to take as much time as you need to feel comfortable before you meet that person. The goal with this communication is to determine if you have enough in common to meet face-to-face. Face-to-face meetings are important because you learn so much more by seeing body language and facial expressions. However, meeting too quickly will not give you sufficient time to screen someone as a potential mate. Spending significantly more than a month e-mailing, texting, and calling may indicate that there is a reluctance to meet and that they may not be an appropriate potential mate.

Taking a year off before dating or only dating casually will allow you to complete a large portion of your emotional healing and re-enter a social life that may have changed since you were last single. This kind of dating will also give you time to figure out what you really want or do not want from your next relationship. As we discussed in chapter 1, you can determine whether you want a serious relationship that will lead to marriage or a relationship that is casual. This will also give you time to really figure out what you are looking for in a mate or partner. After having been married, it is easy to know what you do not want, but it is really important to get in touch with yourself and know what you do want. Once the divorce has ended, take into account that the pain and loss are part of the healing process but not a part of life every day forever. Accept invitations to parties, go out with friends, and stop and talk to strangers, because you never know when or how someone will enter your life.

If you start dating someone who is newly divorced, you must understand that they need time to heal and grow too. One of the most common comments Rick received shortly after his divorce was, "Oh, fresh meat!" People were not far from wrong with those comments. And those comments came from women who had been divorced for at least five to ten years. They already knew what he was about to learn and what he had yet to go through. It is wise to allow all divorced individuals one or more years to date freely before settling down into a serious monogamous relationship. This will save you from heartache and hurt. There are so many stories of people thinking they have met their soul mate only to discover they were dating someone too soon after a divorce. Expectations are unreal at that time and hearts get broken. Give someone time, and if he or she is truly your soul mate, you will find a way to be together.

Red flags with divorced dating:

- Your date compares you to their ex.

- Your date talks about old loves and relationships and does not focus on developing a new relationship with you. They seek to re-create what was in the past. This should be a clue that they are not ready for a relationship but are still hanging on to something that is long gone.

- If they express anger toward his or her ex, others that they have dated, or they are still grieving, it's best to limit the dating to short term.

- Your date ignores or has abandoned their children. This is most common, but not exclusive, among men. This is indicative of poor character, and this person is not someone you want to spend *any* significant time with.

Another aspect that may have taken you by surprise is that some of your friendships will change after divorce. Some friends will remain close to both you and your ex. Some will be friends with you and others will chose to spend their time with your ex. This is common. Those people that chose not to be in your life anymore have chosen for their own reasons. They more than likely were not your best friends and only had loose ties to you because of the relationship they have with your ex. You only want to keep the friends that want to be with you. They are the ones that you will be able to count on in a time of need. In many situations, over time, your married friends will tend to drift away, or you will drift away from them since they remain a couple and you are single. Much of the fun you enjoyed as couples is not quite as fun when you are single. You will find alternate activities in your role as a single person. As you start dating and move into a relationship, you will naturally gravitate back to couples activities again. In the meantime, learn to enjoy your single life. You have to rebuild your social life and support system in a brand new way as a single. For some, it is a significant learning curve to get back into the single life, especially if you had been married for a long time.

Don't hang on to your divorce, your ex, or any other aspect of your divorce. We have all met people who have horror stories about failed relationships and marriages. There is nothing worse than a date telling horror stories about their ex. If these stories are revealed through reasonable, probing questions, then more than likely these people are dealing well with the past. They will more than likely not show significant emotion when telling their story because there has been healing. Then there are those that have to tell their story to every person they meet. They display great emotion, such as anger, hate, and great sadness. These are the people who should not be considered seriously for long-term relationships at this time. Their pain may be too fresh, and they still need time to heal. Others may be hanging on to their anger, hate, or pain for revenge, and you may want to avoid them as a potential mate. They may actually need to seek professional counseling.

Dealing with ex-spouses

This is another area of conversation that needs to be dealt with. You and your mate need to decide on the appropriate time to have a conversation with an ex-spouse. If you have children, don't rely on your children to inform your ex-spouse of your relationship, upcoming engagement, or marriage. This is something you need to do personally. Ex-spouses can create a lot of problems for a new relationship, or any relationship, for that matter. They can also be quite accommodating, depending on your situation. If you are dating someone who has an ex-spouse who has and will continue to create a lot of drama in your life, your mate's life, and the children's lives, you may want to consider gracefully stepping out of this relationship if you are not willing to put up with and deal with their issues. Dating someone with that kind of baggage is difficult. The drama will only get worse in marriage. If this is a relationship that you really want to be in, be aware that the ex-spouse is part of the package, along with ex-in-laws, friends, etc.

Widow/widower

Widows and widowers have a different type of relationship readiness baggage. They have lost their mate through no choice of their own. This can be a devastating loss, especially if they have had a great or extraordinary marriage. Oftentimes they are encouraged to start dating long before they are ready. This encouragement usually comes from very well-meaning family or friends. Rarely do family and friends understand the grief that their loved one is going through. They just want them to find happiness again. Unfortunately, grief needs to run its course and the widow/widower needs time to heal and grow. This kind of healing is similar to that of divorce, discussed above. Widows/widowers just need more time to heal. The experience of grieving the death of a spouse is typically much longer than most people think. It is not uncommon for this process for women to take five years or more. For men it may be a somewhat shorter time frame. I know this may sound like a long time, and for some people it is. However, it is realistic for most people. The loss of a spouse is a huge adjustment that is associated with change and stress. Time is needed to move through the healing process.

One of the true signs that a widow/widower is not emotionally ready to date is that they are still wearing their wedding ring. This is an indication that they are still strongly connected to the past and are not ready to move on. One of the most amazing things is that they may not even be aware that they are still wearing the ring. It is a natural part of their daily life and probably has been for many years prior. It is not until the rings come off that they are starting to make progress toward dating, and even then there is a significant way to go. Other signs of progress are clearing out closets and dressers of the late spouse's clothes, along with giving away or selling jewelry and tools. There are other examples, but you get the point.

Widows/widowers will often talk about their late husband or wife. These can be very unsettling conversations for someone who has never experienced such a loss. You might begin to think that you are being compared to the late spouse. You should not take offense or worry about this kind of discussion or talk unless it becomes excessive. The deceased spouse was very much a part of the person's life and influenced them through all the years of their relationship.

Currently separated

This can be a touchy subject for some people. We are pretty definitive about this. If you are currently separated, the person you want to date is currently separated, or both, *don't date!* The person that is currently separated is *not available!* They (or you) are still married. Do not compound an already difficult situation by committing adultery. Besides the obvious adultery issues that dating a separated person creates, there may be legal issues that come into play. You or your potential mate could be named in divorce/legal proceedings as the cause or a contributing factor in breaking up a marriage. Attorneys can have a field day with this type of information, especially if there is a significant amount of money at stake. It is best to not get involved with anyone until after the divorce is final. If you don't believe us, talk to any good divorce attorney to find out what the negative impact can be to you and your potential mate.

One of the major rules of finding your soul mate is that you and your mate have to be legally and emotionally available to begin a relationship and discover if they are your soul mate. They will not be available until they are divorced. And then, as we mentioned earlier, there is still a healing, growing, and changing period that he or she needs to go through. If this person is truly your soul mate, they will still be your soul mate after they are divorced and have had some time to heal and grow.

Extended families

Whenever you are entering into a new long-term relationship, you will start to meet your mate's family. If your relationship is to be an extraordinary one, these family members will become your extended family. There are a lot of dynamics that will take place here. You may be compared to past spouses or significant others, for better or worse. God forbid you should be caught in a situation where the extended family thought the world of a previous mate and you don't measure up. This should be a red flag, because your mate will more than likely get continuous pressure to get rid of you because you don't measure up to their standards.

Observing the dynamics of your mate's immediate family—parents, brothers, and sisters—will also give you some insight into your mate. How does the family function together? Are they positive and upbeat? Are they negative and do they have a complaint about almost everything? Or are they somewhere in between? As you observe situations, events, or simple gatherings of the extended family, you will need to start to determine whether you fit into their world and vice versa. If you intend to be in a long-term, committed relationship or marriage with your mate, you have to understand that the extended family is part of the package.

Serial dating

Serial dating is a phenomenon that occurs when one has been divorced or widowed for an extended period of time and is not truly willing to commit to another long-term relationship. Most commonly what happens is that the serial dater will make a partial commitment to a relationship and then, after two to four years, leave the relationship. This person will then move on to another relationship, and another, and another. It would appear that after the infatuation has subsided and the routine of normal daily life sets in, the serial dater becomes bored or nervous about a commitment and moves on.

When you start to get to know a person and discover they have had multiple intermediate-term relationships (two to five years) and left for reasons such as "I got bored," "there was no excitement left in our relationship," or "he or she no longer interested me," red flags should go up. This is a person who may not be able to commit to another relationship due to unresolved issues with his or her ex-spouse or may be unwilling to commit wholeheartedly to another relationship for fear of being hurt. Being open and vulnerable is crucial to the success of an extraordinary relationship. Without taking a chance of being hurt, you will never be open enough to commit yourself fully to a relationship. Being guarded and afraid puts up walls or roadblocks in your ability and your mate's ability to build a relationship and get to know each other in a meaningful way.

For many people, opening up emotionally is a huge commitment and an extreme risk. We have all been hurt in the past, and we have to be willing to be hurt again. It is *never* fun and it is *never* easy to be hurt. Without taking this risk, though, we can never move forward in our dating lives, and we run the risk of not only becoming a serial dater, but also missing out on our soul mate.

Cautions for all relationship types

Beware of individuals who are not in touch with who they are and what they do and do not like. Often when people are out of touch with themselves, they will seek to change you or to manipulate you. You will never be appreciated for what or who you are, and you will never be able to make them happy. This is because they themselves do not know what brings happiness. The pressure with this type of relationship will wear you down over time. In discussions with both men and women who have been in long-term relationships, including marriage, they say that "one day it was over." Upon asking why, the initial answer is "I don't know." As you dig deeper and ask them to think about it and look back to the early days of the relationship, they consistently saw that there were problems almost from the start. Yet they stayed in the relationship in spite of the difficulties. Some stay because they don't think the issues are that important. Some stay because they think things will change.

A woman Rick met in the process of writing this book told him that she thought she had found a great guy. She was living with him, and while cohabiting she met another man. This second man decided to leave his wife for her because he thought she was his soul mate. Once he left his wife, he never spoke to his wife again. It took about three years of pursuing this woman, and she finally left the man she was living with. Initially as they dated, things seemed to be going well. They enjoyed many of the same things, including going to church. Shortly after moving in together, he stopped going to church with her. She also found out they had different values when it came to money. After about ten years of living together, the fellow announced that he had found someone else that was his soul mate. Just as with his ex-wife, he has not talked to her since he moved out. The importance of this story is that there were clues all along the way for this woman to observe. One was that the man never spoke to his wife again. Another was that his behavioral patterns changed after they moved in together. The key is to observe what people do and not necessarily what they say. Words can be cheap and may have no meaning unless they are backed up by action.

Involve your children in your decision to date

There is a lot to take into consideration when children are involved in a relationship. One of the first things to consider is whether the children are ready for you to date someone. Children have experienced a great loss, whether it is through divorce or death. They have had no control of the situation, and a huge issue they are dealing with is the fear of loss of the second parent. It may seem irrational but, if you start dating, they will have to give up some of their time with you. The child views the potential mate as competition for your time. This is especially true with younger children. Conversations need to be had with the children to discover their feelings about you dating. They need to know that they are a part of that decision-making process. One of the worst things a parent can do is date, fall in love with someone, and announce a marriage without the children being an integral part of that decision. Because children's thought processes and emotions are so very different from those of adults, they have the ability to seriously impair if not destroy what could have been an extraordinary relationship. They need to be included in the decision-making process right from the beginning. A wonderful book that covers this subject in great detail is *Dating and the Single Parent*, by Ron L. Deal. In it, he discusses many of the common issues of blending families and how to address them for best results.

If your children are not ready for you to date, don't dismiss their concerns. Listen to them and assure them that their concerns are important. It could be that their concerns are so deep that it may be best for you to wait to start dating and seek counseling until they become more accepting. Dating may even have to wait until they become adults and are on their own. Even then, as young adults, their concerns should be addressed, because bringing someone new into their lives will have a significant impact. Issues that need to be addressed include family traditions, holidays, and other special occasions.

Oftentimes children will desire that Mom and Dad reunite. They do not understand that their parents' relationship is over. It may actually be several years before children come to this realization. While you can help your child understand that this is healthy for you, it may not be healthy for the child. If a new mate is introduced into their lives too quickly, they may rebel emotionally and create problems for the new relationship by not accepting the new mate. Do not bring your dates home to meet the kids and do not take them on dates with you until you are well into the relationship and are both serious about a long-term relationship with each other. Children are easily confused, develop attachments quickly, and suffer the consequences of loss. The key here is to not move too quickly and to have good open and honest communication with your children. If they are not ready for Mom or Dad to start dating, then don't. Consider seeking counseling for them and yourself. And if you feel that you must date for your own personal reasons, do so with the understanding that you shouldn't plan on a committed relationship until your children are nearing the end of or are out of high school. Your children should be your first priority. As children mature and are old enough to start dating themselves, they may come to realize that the custodial parent may want and should have someone in their life too.

Red flags of poor manners

Men, one thing that should set off a red flag is when a woman becomes upset with you for being a gentleman. Rick has heard several stories and had several experiences with these types of situations. Recently a divorced friend was recounting a story of a date he had. He explained that he was being a gentleman, opening her car door, the restaurant door, letting her order her meal first, practicing old-fashioned courtesy and manners. He said that they seemed to have a decent time, and as they got back into his car, he opened her door and then he got in on the driver's side. He no sooner got his door closed than she started to berate him for opening her door. She said she was independent and completely capable of opening and closing her own doors and did not need his help. This is a huge difference in thinking and values, and it should be a red flag if there is anger or dissatisfaction expressed at offering up a common courtesy and showing manners. Some women consider it insulting to their feminine values to be doted upon with opening doors, helping her with putting on or taking off her coat, and good old-fashioned manners. Men, if you like catering to a woman in this way, look for those women who enjoy and appreciate old-fashioned values.

Another question on manners came from a female friend on Facebook. She posted an open question to all her friends and asked: If a man is acting like a gentleman, opens the door, and lets you go first, is he really being a gentleman, or is he just trying to get a look at your assets? Rick was somewhat relieved to see that most of the responses affirmed that the man was in fact being a gentleman. Penny felt that this question was silly to post. Of course the man will check out the woman's assets, just as the woman is checking out his. That is why you are on a date. No matter who goes first or last, checking each other out is what dating is all about. Early in a relationship, this is a natural part of determining physical attraction. When you like or love someone, you appreciate what you see coming and going. Gentlemen who let the woman go first do not have the sole motive to check out her assets, but to be considerate and demonstrate manners. When a man takes a woman's hand and leads her through a rough crowd, does she check him out? You bet she does. However, this is not the sole reason she allows him to lead. Most women like to feel protected and safe, and allowing the man to lead the way in a large crowd is one way for him to demonstrate that protection. Not all women appreciate protection, but instead feel that they can take care of themselves. This is a big value difference and cannot be reconciled quickly or easily. It is best to consider the differences respectfully and find someone who shares the same value structure as you.

Finally, Rick recounted an event, "I was out with a friend for an evening of dancing. As I walked around her to open her door, she said; 'Don't you dare open my door. I don't want anyone to think we are dating or that we are a couple.' I opened her door anyway. We had a discussion about men opening doors for women and that it was the polite thing to do and had nothing to do with whether we were a couple or not. She did apologize, but the point is that she didn't think it appropriate for a man to open a door unless they were dating." Gifts of service are not always appreciated by everyone, and it is important when giving that gift that the other person enjoys or appreciates the gift. This strengthens the relationship and helps you to grow together as a couple.

It is amazing what an impact the feminist movement has had on our society and the role confusion it has created. Men and women have a broad spectrum of values and expectations. Communication is foundational in discovering these expectations and values. Examples of this are that men can be berated by women for being a gentleman, and then the women will turn around and complain that there are no good men out there. In today's society, a woman can be expected to work outside the home, cook, and run a household, and the man wonders why she is not excited to see him. It is universal that a man needs to feel appreciated and wanted by a woman, and vice versa. A man cannot feel appreciated and wanted if he is berated for being a gentleman. A woman cannot feel attracted to a man who is insincere and rude. All men should aspire to be gentlemen and be polite and courteous. All ladies should aspire to be with gentlemen who respect and value them for who they are.

Ending a non marriage relationship

When you end a relationship, end it! You can be polite and cordial in public, but don't stay in regular or continual contact with your ex-partner. When you end a relationship (or have a relationship ended on you), move on. Lose his or her phone number, e-mail address, and any other contact information if you are tempted to contact them. It may be a good idea to leave them in your data base so you know not to answer their call or text. This is especially true if one of you is the "clingy" type or if you are the type of person who wants to be liked by everyone. You cannot remain friends with everyone, no matter how much you would like to. Don't answer phone calls, text messages, or e-mails once the relationship is over. The minute you answer a call, e-mail, or text, you open the door to further communication, regardless of whether that is your intention or not. Do not hold on to a relationship that is now extinct.

As a side note, if you are breaking off all contact with someone, please have the maturity and courtesy to tell them that you want no more contact. Do not let someone leave phone messages, write e-mails, or send text messages for several days or weeks and hope that they will get the hint that you have no intention of responding. You may try to justify this to yourself by saying you don't want to hurt his or her feelings. This is a coward's way out. It may be a difficult step for you to take, but it needs to be done.

If you are hesitant to end a relationship because you don't want to hurt someone's feelings, take note. You have no control over anyone's feelings but your own. You can influence someone's feelings only if they let you, and it is their choice, not yours, to let you do so. This point was driven home to Rick several years ago when his college-age daughter was home for Easter. She said she wanted to join us for church Easter morning. Easter morning came and it was time to start getting ready for church. I woke my daughter up several times, and it took a lot of effort to get her up and going. Anyone who knows my daughter knows that she is not a morning person. She begrudgingly got up and got dressed. When we finally got into the car, she slammed her door closed. I looked at her and in a very stern voice asked what her problem was, reminding her that she was the one who said she wanted to join us for church. She replied with a snide tone, "You are my problem! You put me in this mood!" I said, "Really? Well, if I control your mood, then I command you to be in a good mood!" The look on her face was priceless. She realized at that very instant that *she* was in control of her emotions. It was only a few minutes later that she became pleasant to be with, and the rest of the day was terrific.

Ending a relationship or setting boundaries within a relationship is something you must do for yourself. You cannot control or change the outcome of how the other person responds. Their feelings are their choice, and you are responsible for your actions and feelings only. Emotions, actions, and feelings are your baggage. Look into your suitcase and see what you have packed. In the next chapter we will help you determine what is healthy and normal, what is not, and eliminate the harmful and unnecessary junk from your trunk.

Chapter 3

Emotional baggage and what
we have packed

In everyday life we face a variety of issues that can create roadblocks and hurdles for any relationship. By understanding what many of these hurdles are, you will be better equipped to recognize and be alert for warning signs that could lead to potentially unhealthy relationships. In this chapter we are going to review a number of very technical subjects. It is not our intent for this information to be a comprehensive study of any of these subjects. It is merely an overview. We encourage you to do further study on all of the subjects presented in this chapter. We have provided a recommended reading list at the end of this book to help guide you in gaining a deeper understanding of some of the information presented here.

Emotional maturity

Judging emotional health can be difficult. It is important to understand that the lack of character or maturity does not constitute emotional illness, but is a reflection of how that individual processes and responds to life situations. Maturity is multifaceted and has the ability to adapt to change. Emotional connections can be difficult based on any one or more of the following subcomponents listed below. As you grow and mature in these areas, it leads to emotional maturity. How your family reacted to emotions—the support they gave, withheld, or lacked—will directly impact how you relate to and feel emotionally toward others. In their book *How We Love*, Milan and Kay Yerkovich discuss five styles of imprinting from your parents that impact how emotions are shared and felt and explain how the imprinting influences your relationships with others. Imprinting impacts relationships of all types. What we will deal with next are the different subtopics that lead to emotional maturity and how to spot red flags from those who are emotionally immature, stunted, or scarred. These are many of the same characteristics that are seen in codependent people. There is one major rule in relationships with emotional immaturity and codependency: *You cannot fix what you did not break.* Each person is responsible for their own maturity, you are the only one that can change, and as a mate you cannot bring their maturity in to existence. If you are in a relationship and both of you are emotionally immature, stunted, or scared, you are probably in a codependent relationship. The problem with this type of relationship is that it typically continues to spiral downward. Both partners feed off of each other's problems, and each sees the other as being at fault. Soul mates are emotionally mature individuals who live and grow through life together, unlike codependents, who tend to tear their relationships and each other apart. Now, let's examine the subcomponents of emotional maturity.

Emotional maturity subcomponents

Dealing with reality constructively

Maturity is demonstrated in the ability to tolerate criticism, search for the truth, accept the truth, and make difficult choices. The essence of dealing with reality constructively is mature, healthy communication. The statement "Honey, do these jeans make me look fat?" is a loaded question. Many battles have begun and relationships have been lost because of the inability to honestly and maturely communicate a response to difficult questions.

Dealing with reality constructively requires mature communication between two people: a sender and a receiver. Each person has the ability to function as both a sender and a receiver. This process can be likened to that of a CB radio antenna. As we speak, we send out a "signal," so we become the sender. The person listening to us receives our "signal" and thus becomes the receiver. Adult communication is spoken respectfully to each other *as* adults. Problems with communication and emotions result when conversations take a parent-child format. The book *I'm OK—You're OK*, written by Thomas A. Harris, outlines communication forms that are immature and unhealthy and those that are healthy.

Healthy communication and dealing with reality begin with adult-to-adult communication and a respect for each other as the sender and receiver. Healthy, mature communication allows messages to be sent and received from one adult to another. Unhealthy communication will leave one or more persons feeling that they are not "OK." As an adult, when someone speaks to you like a parent, or you are feeling like a child being spoken to, it is an indication that communication is unhealthy. Maturity allows us to hear the truth and be respectful and responsible in dealing with the truth to promote growth in the relationship. Sometimes when truth is spoken, it is difficult to hear, even for the most emotionally mature person. No one has ever been heard to say, "Tell me again how I am inadequate and at fault." We all want to be loved for who we are.

A difficult topic that impacts dealing with reality constructively is abuse. It has been said that one in three of the general population is known to experience abuse on some level. This abuse can be physical, verbal, emotional, or sexual; it can be neglect; or it can be some combination of these. It is thought that this number may be even higher due to the lack of reporting. Abuse will stunt and damage the emotional responsiveness and the ability to deal with reality in the abuse victim. Abuse causes feelings of fear, reprisal, disrespect, and dishonor in those who suffer the abuse. The negative emotions associated with abuse create complex emotional damage and difficulty dealing with reality and truth. It distorts how relationships are viewed and the feelings relationships create.

A basic human need is to love and be loved. The lack of positive emotional support and love in an abusive and highly critical communication style, coupled with unrealistic expectations, will create anxiety, fears, worry, and anger that can manifest itself in a variety of different ways. It can range from the strong need to be liked by everyone and please people to deep depression. The effects can cause mixed feelings of intense desire to be with a person, followed by the need to then push away. There is a vast difference between a healthy relationship, where you want to meet your mate's needs or desires, and trying to please someone through a dysfunctional relationship. The reality is that our emotional upbringing impacts our lifelong emotional expectations. Unless the individual deals with an unhealthy, abusive past directly, they are very likely to remain trapped in a cycle of unhealthy relationships.

Searching for a mate that we connect with emotionally requires dealing with both reality and truth constructively. Dealing with emotions should always be born out of love.

Mature love:

- Is long suffering, bears annoyances and inconveniences, and does not lose its temper.

- Is kind, taking the initiative to be considerate and helpful.

- Does not envy but rejoices when the other has success.

- Is not prideful or puffed up.

- Does not act rudely or impolitely.

- Does not seek its own way but always seeks to benefit others.

- Allows for differences of opinion in minor matters.

- Thinks no evil and makes allowances for people's flaws.

- Does not rejoice in iniquity, but rejoices in the truth.

None of us is perfect in this lifetime, and mature people make the decision to love their mates. This includes loving them with the flaws that make them unique. They will deal with the large issues through caring, tenderness, and love. Mature individuals are able to admit wrong, forgive, and go on loving.

"Truth delivered outside of love and caring is a form of abuse."
—*Penny Dunning*

In your search for the mate who is perfect for you, it is wise to understand that humans are not perfect and will never respond perfectly in this life. The mature emotional mate will be able to deal with reality constructively with a decision to love.

Ability to adapt to change

Life brings challenges daily and opportunities to change and grow. All living things grow, and nothing that is alive will stay the same. Growth means life. In business it is often said, "If you aren't growing, you're dying." Healthy relationships are dynamic, not static. This means that the relationship will (and has to) evolve over time. All growth and change involves taking some risk and accepting some discomfort. Here are some very common and very valid questions about change, along with some answers.

- *"What if I fail?"* And what if you succeed? You can only fail if you don't try. If your attempts are not successful at first, learn what doesn't work, make changes, and try again.

- *"What if I make the change and I don't like the results?"* Then change again, and keep changing until you get the positive results you want.

- *"What if I'm not accepted if I make these changes?"* We always want to be accepted, but let's make sure we are accepted by the right people. If you are not accepted by your existing circle of friends or colleagues, then they are probably the wrong people to have in your life if you are doing the right things.

- *"What if people laugh or make fun of me?"* People have laughed and scoffed at great people throughout history. If you believe in what you are doing and know that it is the right thing to do, then keep doing it. The laughers and scoffers will eventually become believers or they will move on.

Now, with all that being said, a certain amount of safety and security is needed for personal and emotional change and growth to occur. We need to feel confident that there is important emotional support for our efforts to change. Youths and young adults are generally more eager to embrace new opportunities, change, and growth potential. The older we become, the more mature we seem to be due to the growth and change that has accumulated in our lifetime. Change does seem to become more difficult and labor intensive as we grow older. The longer you live, the more likely it is that your soul mate requirement list will be more specific and longer. Age brings experience, insight, wisdom, and less likelihood to change. Youth brings an eagerness to explore, learn, and change with a flexibility that allows growth in many directions. A red flag for relationships is to be completely unwilling to make any change and inflexible without consideration for one's mate. This rigidity is not a sign of mature emotional health or strong values, but rather of immaturity, no matter what the age.

We want to be clear here that we are not talking about changing or being overly flexible with your morals or your core values. (Core values will be discussed later in this chapter.) Morals can be simply defined as knowing the difference between right and wrong. However, in our society today, we are seeing a breakdown of moral values and what is acceptable as right and wrong. This topic alone can be the subject of an entire book. Suffice it to say that if your family was socially accepted as normal, your parent(s) probably instilled basic moral values in you that help guide you in determining right from wrong.

Ability to make long-range choices

Long-range choices are those for which we need the discipline to postpone immediate gratification for the greater benefit of future results. The ability to delay gratification or delay immediate pleasure to attain a long-term goal is a sign of maturity. Seeking pleasure here and now without concern for the future is a sign of immaturity. Poor choices are a result of immature decision-making ability. Poor decisions that could have an adverse impact on the future might include the choice to smoke or be smoke free. It could be the choice of having a candy bar for a snack or an apple. It could be taking money out of your 401(k) or IRA to buy a boat instead of saving for it. It could be spending your tax refund on a big-screen TV or a cruise instead of your child's education. In a relationship, it could be postponing physical intimacy until marriage. We will make an infinite number of choices in our lifetime. Not all of them will be good, but the more we focus on our long-term goals and desires, the more likely we are to achieve them.

If you have rarely (if ever) delayed immediate gratification in preference for your long-term needs and goals, take heart. You can change. It takes a conscious effort and becomes gradually easier with each positive decision you make. Postponing immediate gratification can become an important way of life after you have had several successes. These are usually small successes at first, and usually one at a time. Continued success is built one step at a time; one success, then another, then another. You will come to feel and appreciate the long-term gratification and joy of knowing that you have achieved something of value to you. You will also have missteps along the way. Don't let temporary setbacks keep you from achieving your long-term goals. Refocus and move forward.

Impulsiveness with money is one of the most common red flags we see and should be addressed early on in your search for a soul mate. Money has been documented to be one the most common factors in marriage disputes. By addressing this issue before you are in a committed relationship, you can help alleviate significant problems in your future. Uncontrolled impulsivity without regard for the future is a big red flag and demonstrates immaturity and the inability to make long-range choices or delay gratification.

Must have a reasonable degree of independence

Small children require assistance and constant nurturing. As babies grow, they begin to explore the world around them. As we move from infant to toddler to adolescent, we gain more and more freedom to explore. As we move through these life stages we gain the ability to make decisions alone and become independent. Life experiences can create fear and a dependency on others, or they can go to the other extreme, in which total independence and isolation can occur. When basic emotional needs as a child are not met or abuse occurs, this can impact how dependent or independent an individual is. Mature relationships have a balance of respect for individual need and dependence. This is called *interdependence.*

Interdependence in a healthy relationship allows one to feel that he or she *wants* to be with their mate but doesn't *need* to be with them. It allows the freedom to have individual activities, hobbies, or interests without requiring your significant other to participate. For women, it is going to lunch or a movie or having a spa day with girlfriends without your mate being jealous. For men, it is a day of golf, hunting, fishing, or poker without your significant other being jealous. Your true soul mate and you will function in an interdependent fashion. It is normal to depend on, want, need, and have love from another person. It is abnormal to disrespect each other's need for their space and time. Men like their man cave and women love their bubble bath time. Intrusion on this personal, individual, private time, or denial of it, is a red flag.

Relationships require a healthy balance of "me" and "us" time. Spending all of your time together in "us" time generally results in a stunting of individuality and personal growth. This will foster a codependent relationship where neither person is fully satisfied. In a codependent relationship, one or both mates have an empty "love tank." Our love tanks are filled when we receive love and are drained when we give love. If we are giving more than we receive, our tanks will be emptied in time. If we come into a relationship with empty love tanks, we have no love to give and thus the relationship suffers greatly and ultimately cannot survive.

As children, we expect our parent(s) to give us the love and attention we need. In dysfunctional families the child's love tank is generally not adequately filled by the parent(s). When one or both parents in a dysfunctional family are not getting the healthy love and attention they need and desire, in many cases, they may turn to the child for love, further draining the child's love tank. This is often referred to as "emotional incest." As the child grows into adulthood, they typically seek love in dysfunctional, codependent relationships. As you can start to see, the codependent relationship can drain an already low love tank...and the spiral continues downward.

Problems that are often seen in codependent relationships are typically socially negative addictions, such as alcohol and drug abuse. However, there are other addictions that have a more positive social acceptance, such as workaholism, eating disorders, an extremely rigid and legalistic approach to living, or maybe even martyrdom. We all appear to understand negative addictions and the impact they have on our mate or significant other. Workaholics may appear to be industrious achiever types, but their efforts may be covering up a deeper problem. It may be that work is the only place they find peace or satisfaction in their lives and may be a substitute for love. Martyrs are usually those significant others that are in relationships with the alcoholic, addict, or workaholic. They may take some satisfaction from the sacrifices that they make to maintain or hold a relationship together. Entering a relationship with a codependent person should give rise to huge red flags right from the start. We all build walls around us. It's natural to help protect us from life's unusual bumps and bruises. Codependents build walls that are thicker and higher than normal. They have issues that need to be addressed and should seek treatment from professionals or trained counselors.

What are your individual passions? What are or could be your shared passions? Life is an adventure to discover those individual and shared passions. When two mature individuals grow independently they can also grow together. There is something mysterious and miraculous that happens when this type of growth occurs. There is a unique transformation that takes place individually and as a couple. Soul mates grow in response to the other's growth, and as a result the relationship grows exponentially. Together you are more than you can be as an individual. Relationships require work from both individuals to balance their "me" and "us" time and make time for both to nurture and grow the soul mate relationship.

Must have concern for other people

A hallmark of maturity and emotional health is having a concern for others. Under ideal conditions, to love others as much as you love yourself would transform the world from one that is filled with hate and crime to utopia. This kind of caring is transformational to a relationship and the individuals it touches. Are you looking for a partner who has sensitivity for your needs? Do you think that they should know your needs before you speak them? The answer to both questions for a soul mate should be yes. We are not saying that you need to be able to read your mate's mind and vice versa. What we are saying is that with the right person, you should have a certain ability to notice facial expressions, look into his or her eyes, and see that twinkle or understand when something is wrong. Developing a concern for the individual and having a mature relationship does not happen quickly or without sacrifice. Understanding what someone wants or needs takes active participation by both partners. It requires an awareness of what is happening within that individual and what he or she likes, needs, or desires at that moment in time. This includes personal needs that can be low key or very intimate.

How is it that someone's needs are met? It begins with good communication, being open, and expressing your needs if they are not "caught" or understood by your mate. Your soul mate should be willing to meet those needs. Loving and giving unconditionally to each other is a must to attain this level of concern and caring. Problems result when emotional immaturity or dysfunction creates an unbalanced give and take that destroys relationships. Continually giving without receiving will drain your love tank. Continual receiving may partially fill your love tank but will be limited by what the giver actually has to offer and how much they can actually give. Both giving without receiving and receiving without giving while also expecting to have your love tank filled are signs of a codependent relationship. True love accepts and appreciates the gifts that are given and does not demand or expect in return. These are not just material gifts, but gifts of self-sacrifice, patience, long-suffering, self-restraint, joy, honesty, service, and all gifts of virtue.

The ability to meet the needs of others requires self-respect, loving yourself, and having insight to others' needs and the willingness to actively meet those needs. Caring can be expressed by simple acts such as holding the door open for your mate, getting him or her a glass of water, or running through the rain to get the car so the "dry clean only" dress does not become ruined. True, honest, mature caring happens without self-gain or expectations. It is given freely and with love. Mature individuals respect others' feelings, taking care not to purposely offend them and to speak truth with kindness. Your choice in a mate will directly impact your happiness and the outcome of your life. The adventure of life and how you care and support each other will impact the success you share as individuals and as a couple.

Relating well to other people requires us to recognize and respect their emotional needs and see beyond ourselves. To ignore, assume, or meddle with their emotions can result in negative outcomes that are not associated with true caring. Look for those that can give as well as receive emotionally, because it is a blessing to give as well as receive. Giving to others allows you to feel the joy of giving, and by receiving you allow others to feel joy of giving to you.

The words we speak and how we speak them are evidence of caring. Adult-to-adult communication does not include lies, insincerity, or hurtful remarks. Communication that contains any of these should raise the red flag of emotional immaturity. Caring can be summed up by a genuine interest in the other person, respect for his or her opinion, sharing genuine compliments, and the belief that they are truly important enough in your eyes that you will put their needs in front of your own in caring for them.

Must have satisfactory relationships with others

Emotional health is demonstrated by the ability to relate to others and work in groups successfully. Developmental psychology has shown that small children play independently and are unable to engage in group play until they mature. This is the struggle that all toddlers face developmentally. Adults who are unable to work in groups are stunted, immature, and will be unsuccessful in long-term individual relationships. Self-confidence is key to being able to work with a group and yet have others feel accepted. If the mate you are considering is unable to work in groups, you should pause to examine his or her attitudes and actions. For example:

- He/she is always right and everyone else is wrong.

- He/she feels rejected when others don't accept his/her ideas.

- He/she gives hostile and inconsiderate responses to others.

These are red flags for emotional immaturity and will result in limited relationship growth and ongoing struggles.

Must be able to work productively

Have you met a person who cannot hold a job for any length of time? They complain that the work is below them, the boss is too demanding, or they cannot meet the daily job requirements. Productive working is a sign of emotional health. Continual trouble completing work assignments or goals can be the result of emotional conflicts. Lack of focus is often a result of emotional conflict. Poor academic success in younger people can often be the result of emotional conflict that goes unresolved. Adults who are chronically unemployed often suffer from emotional problems that impair the ability to interview for jobs successfully or attain goals for success.

The importance of values

Values are indicative of a person's philosophy for living and are influenced by where you live, the era of birth, parents' values, friends' values, school experiences, religious beliefs, and everything else that can impact the individual's life. It cannot be stated strongly enough that parenting styles and parental values directly impact our emotional connectedness to others. Finding the soul mate that has virtues means finding a person actively living by their values, and this is more precious than gold and silver. Some core values that demonstrate a willingness to put others ahead of self are:

VALUES			
Accountability	Balance	Courage	Creative
Discipline	Faith	Fairness	Family
Friendship	Generous	Harmony	Health
Hope	Humility	Joy	Love
Loyal	Open	Patience	Reliability
Respect	Responsible	Security	Sharing
Sincere	Thoughtfulness	Trust	Humor

It is important to understand that your values should be in alignment with each other. This can be a significant factor in the success or failure of a relationship. Without having similar values, you bring potential conflict into the future of your relationship. Very few people we know can have an extraordinary relationship if their values are not aligned. When these values are in alignment and put into action, it creates energy in a relationship that nurtures the soul. A hallmark sign of a potential soul mate are many shared values. Mature individuals draw on the experiences of others, find and integrate all that holds meaning, respect others who differ, and re-evaluate personal values as life progresses.

Stress and emotions

Emotions cannot be discussed without touching on the topic of stress. Hans Selye is a Canadian physiologist who defines stress in a general way. It is defined as a group of changes in a living system that produce external or internal force. Emotional stress is often associated with negative consequences, such as fatigue, fear, physical illness, anxiety, depression, anger, frustration, or tension, to name a few. Relationships that are mismatched, codependent, or emotionally immature can result in negative, stress-producing life events, such as physical illness, spiritual illness (getting mad at God, losing faith, etc.), psychological disorders, and physical abuse, just to name a few.

Your body responds to stress with a physical response regardless of whether the stress is real or imagined. For instance, if a man pulls a gun and holds it to your head, your body will cause a response known as the "fight or flight syndrome." Your heartbeat increases, you begin to sweat, your hands might shake, your knees feel weak, and a wave of nausea and impending doom occurs. You will want to stand up and fight or run and hide from what is causing the stress. The gun is very real, and the response your body gives will increase your awareness and ability to deal with the situation.

The same physiological response can be triggered from a thought or negative treatment within a relationship. When stress occurs daily in a relationship, a strain and a demand are placed on the body, causing it to become weakened. The impact to the immune system is such that it cannot continue to function at a high level, and disease takes over due to a weakened and exhausted defense system. Stress that is not managed well will result in increased illness, disease, depression, and anxiety.

General Adaptation Syndrome is how we deal with stress daily through our coping mechanisms. Avoidance is the most common form of coping. We will go out of our way to not place ourselves in the presence of that which creates stress. This coping is common and helpful on a short-term basis. An "avoidance" form of coping becomes negative when it continues long term. In the most intense form, it is known as a phobia. For some individuals, avoidance becomes severe enough that they will not leave their home or participate in social gatherings in order to avoid stressful situations or relationships.

Denial

Denial is another common form of coping used to protect the ego and emotions by refusing to acknowledge that a stressful situation exists. Refusing to see, hear, or recognize stress is a process known as "tuning out." When a person chooses to deny stress, this creates the perception that stress does not exist, and it is protection for the ego and emotions. It allows an avoidance of reality and responsibility for dealing with the stress that exists in the life of the person at that moment in time. Creation of this denial perception can be unconscious or intentional, and temporarily helpful or permanently harmful. Relationships suffer a loss of emotional connectedness and intimacy when denial is used to cope with stress. Denial creates walls that keep honest, open communication from happening. The result is that individual needs are not met and the relationship grows apart instead of closer.

Denial can result in many arguments and inhibit growth in relationships. The example of denial that is being presented here is a difficult issue that has resulted in the destruction of emotional connections in many relationships. It is our hope that your communication as an individual and within a relationship will be improved and increased, security in each other will grow, emotional intimacy will be fostered, and there will be less use of denial after having digested this information.

Men and women think and process emotions differently, and their brains respond through different pathways to create emotions and thoughts. Men are primarily stimulated visually, and women are primarily stimulated with thoughts. When a beautiful woman catches the eye of a man, he may follow her across the room with his eyes. A woman who catches her man with this look in his eye will feel insecure and wonder if he is planning on leaving her, what he sees in her, and how she compares to that woman. If they are on the first date or two, red flags should be waving in front of the woman's face.

This is not a man who has total interest in you. Consider ending the date right then and there and move on to someone who will focus all of his attention on you. However, men do not think these thoughts to hurt the one they are with; it just happens as a response to the stimulus. This is not an excuse or license for all men to ogle and lust after women openly. This is an attempt to help women understand what happens in the male mind and how it is different from the female mind. If the relationship continues along this path, emotional walls start to develop, and the budding relationship starts to shut down. This is how denial creates an emotional wall and separation begins for an individual and within a relationship.

Denial can manifest itself in other ways also. We both have seen countless examples of men and women in denial of their emotional readiness to date after a divorce or the death of a spouse. As we discussed in chapter 2, people who are recently widowed or divorced have a significant amount of healing and growing to do. This process can generally take from one to five years on average. If you enter into a relationship too soon with someone who is newly widowed or divorced, you should quickly see red flags alerting you to problems that you will most likely want to avoid.

Denial can also manifest itself in self-denial of physical appearance, health, personal abilities, or habits. I (Rick) have personally spent time with a woman that denied she had a weight issue. At nearly one hundred pounds overweight, in her mind she still saw herself as "about average" and only had a few pounds to lose. It made no difference what I told her or how encouraging I was when she did try to diet; she still saw herself as "about average." It wasn't until she changed her internal self-image that she was finally able to lose weight. Other examples might be thinking that you can run a 5K or 10K race when you are thirty pounds overweight and don't even jog to the corner of the street, or of trying to wear clothes you wore twenty years ago when they clearly don't fit or make you look completely out of touch with fashion reality. Just because they looked good back then doesn't mean they look good on you now.

Up to this point, most of the denial we have talked about is dealing with people in their forties and fifties. For those of you who are in your twenties or thirties, your issues may be different. Because of a certain lack of life experiences, you may not immediately recognize various forms of denial. A common denial with you may be cell phone addiction. We have all seen people out socializing and many of them will be continuously texting someone else. If you are out on a date and the person you are with cannot put the phone down for more than a couple of minutes at a time, they may have a serious addiction problem. Their attention should be on you and you only. Unless they have young children with a baby sitter, are a doctor on call, or the White House has them on speed dial, they have no business giving attention to anyone but you. They may even deny having an addiction problem. If he or she refuses to turn the phone off or put it away, and you stay for the rest of the date, you may be in denial of recognizing that a problem exists.

The truth can be hard to hear and requires mature individuals to communicate openly and honestly. For this to happen, you must have a safe person in your life in whom you can confide and to whom you are willing to listen. This "safe" person could be a close friend, pastor, or counselor. Your soul mate should be your safe haven and safe place to share the truth. Problems result in relationships when there is emotional overload and denial. Feelings of neglect or unimportance happen when truthful communication is lacking or there is the inability to face truth because denial exists. Communication doors that were once open become closed to emotional connections and intimacy. The loss of emotional connections and intimacy create barriers for growth and create decay in the relationship. Feeling safe and being open to respectful communication within a relationship are foundational for healthy stress management.

So where and how is denial seen within a relationship? An example would be that we all have deep feelings, emotional connections, hopes, and desires in life. When these deep desires become threatened, it is easy to pretend that the threat does not exist to keep these feelings intact. Denial of inner feelings and emotions can be directed toward other people or material things that you possess. When there is no chance of attaining your heart's desire for emotional connections, ownership of material things, or intimacy, negative communication is usually the result. When a deep hope, feeling, connection, or emotion is blocked or threatened, you will often witness criticism and ridicule. We have all seen a young man or woman who falls head over heels for someone of the opposite sex. If the same emotions are not reciprocated, you will hear the person say, "Well, they are so stuck up!" or "What do you expect when they cannot see what they are missing by not liking or loving me. They are dumber than dirt." Negativism and criticism are common types of expressions when emotional walls are erected from denial.

Regression and fixation

Intense stress can result in regression, or going back to a behavior from an earlier stage of life. Stress that is extremely intense can cause an adult to become baby-like in behavior and actions. In extreme cases the regression can be so severe that there is a loss of bodily functions, or the person will not eat unless fed and will lie around crying. A less severe form of regression can be seen when a divorce occurs and there is a moving home to live with the parents and allowing the parents to take care of the divorced person's needs. Penny had an uncle who, after he divorced, lived at her grandparents' home. His bed was the living room couch in their home until the day he died. Adults should be fully able to meet their own needs, but through regression they seek to have others provide their care and support. Fixation is closely associated with regression. The difference is that maturation never takes place, and the fixated person remains emotionally immature and fixed in time. These are the people you meet who you feel never grew up and are stuck in their teens and twenties. Mature relationships are generally not possible with them.

Sublimation

A healthy form of dealing with stress is sublimation. This is a transformation of stressful energy into positive channels or activities. This will strengthen the individual as stress is transformed. Finding positive outlets for this stress can be as simple as volunteering to help mow your neighbor's lawn, exercise, creative outlets, such as oil painting, woodworking, photography, restoring old cars, etc., or cleaning a room from top to bottom.

Compulsive behavior

The opposite of sublimation is compulsive behavior. This is a mechanical response to avoid punishment for a negative behavior. An example is when a child could have been punished for laziness, messiness, carelessness, or any other behavior the parental value system deemed necessary. To avoid punishment, the individual may compulsively clean to the point it will rob him or her of happiness because everything revolves around cleanliness. Compulsions can negatively impact relationships when combined with fear and unrealistic expectations of a partner. As stated earlier, when harmful behaviors develop in dealing with stress, you see repeating patterns. The most common patterns of compulsion are excessive eating, spending, alcohol use, drug use, and sexual addictions. Eating, smoking, and chewing gum will help reduce tension, but can have some negative impact if this is the sole source of comfort. Alcohol and drugs work to reduce stress, but dull the senses and ability to resolve the issues in a healthy, permanent way. Used in excess, these "stress reducers" can become addictions that mask the underlying problem and ultimately become a problem of their own. There are times where self-help books and courses will assist in overcoming compulsive behaviors, while some will require professional assistance.

Stress: the good and the bad

This one word, *stress*, will immediately bring positive and negative feelings to the surface. Stress is a natural part of daily living, and within the next two sections we will discuss the impact of stress on your relationships. Signs that stress is present can be illness, emotional or physical growth limitations, fighting, or fleeing. Our natural defense mechanism is triggered as a response to stress, and it occurs for all situations, real or imagined. We will begin to explore the emotional connections and negative impact of stress and finish up with why positive stress is needed.

Negative stress

Stress results from the environment, the physical body, and the mind. Stress becomes negative when the outcomes create damage or become toxic. Excess stress can take on many forms, such as staying overactive to avoid conflict, resulting in a lack of time and poor self-reflection skills. It is necessary to have some "quiet time." So often when we are dealing with stress, which can manifest itself as loneliness, anxiety, depression, or other emotions, it can negatively occupy our time by excessive shopping, exercising, spending time with friends and family, or other activities. While there may be nothing inherently wrong with these legal activities, if they are being used to avoid feelings, these choices can be detrimental to understanding why the stress exists and what you are feeling. We were given emotions for a reason. When you have strong feelings or emotions, it is advisable to take some time, preferably alone, to figure out what you are feeling and why you are feeling this way. Emotions are signals telling us we need to be aware of something. If we don't know what we feel, we don't know what we need. Here are a few questions to get you started on this process.

- What are the emotions I am feeling right now?

  Just a few examples are feeling bored, distressed, apprehensive, terrified, hurt, lost, angered, enraged, frustrated, sad, disappointed, guilty, regretful, inadequate, unworthy, overwhelmed, depressed, and lonely.

- Why am I feeling these emotions?

- How do I want to feel?

- What would I have to do or believe to feel that way?

- What can I learn from this negative feeling to avoid feeling like this in the future?

Depending on the resources you check, it is claimed that there are as many as four thousand words in the English language that describe emotions. Here are a few, categorized first by positive and negative feelings and listed by a general emotion that is underlined.

Positive Feelings			
<u>OPEN</u>	HAPPY	ALIVE	GOOD
understanding	gay	playful	calm
sympathetic	joyous	courageous	peaceful
reliable	fortunate	energetic	at ease
easy	delighted	liberated	comfortable
kind	ecstatic	frisky	relaxed
accepting	festive	thrilled	certain
satisfied	gleeful	impulsive	encouraged
LOVE	INTERESTED	POSITIVE	STRONG
considered	fascinated	determined	unique
affectionate	intrigued	excited	dynamic
tender	absorbed	enthusiastic	tenacious
devoted	inquisitive	eager	impulsive
passionate	snoopy	keen	hardy
sensitive	curious	iIntent	certain

Negative Feelings			
ANGRY	DEPRESSED	CONFUSED	HELPLESS
irritated	lousy	upset	incapable
enraged	disappointed	doubtful	alone
Insulting	ashamed	indecisive	fatigued
unpleasant	miserable	hesitant	vulnerable
offensive	detestable	skeptical	empty
bitter	repugnant	stupefied	forced
aggressive	despicable	disillusioned	hesitant
INDIFFERENT	AFRAID	HURT	SAD
provoked	fearful	distrustful	distressed
nonchalant	scared	misgiving	woeful
neutral	sulky	crushed	sorrowful
weary	terrified	unsure	tragic
disinterested	panic	pained	tearful
lifeless	frightened	aching	grieved

Use these words to prompt you to think about what you are actually feeling. If you are feeling negative emotions or feelings, use the questions above to help you address your feelings.

Negative stress and repression

Relationships experience stress as changes in life occur. You can expect continued drama and added anxiety in a relationship when a memory, an event, or a feeling is blocked from the conscious mind but continues to have influence. This is known as repression. One example of this can be seen when a woman who is sexually abused as a child will block those memories. The abuse continues to influence how she relates to men and her relationships to others and even to her own children because of her creation of emotional walls. We naturally have emotional walls due to life's everyday turmoil. The walls become higher and wider when emotional abuse is involved. Physical walls can also be erected in a variety of ways, such as eating disorders when one gains excessive weight, poor personal hygiene, or the extension of personal space boundaries. Professional help may be necessary to resolve repressed conflicts. Failure to deal with repressed negative emotions can result in anxiety, excess drama, and depression. This anxiety and drama in your life will negatively impact you and limit the emotional growth potential for you and all of your interpersonal relationships.

Negative stress and projection

Have you ever experienced an outright lie and then had that lie blamed on you? You know you are innocent and are left wondering, what on earth is all that about? Projection attempts to manage anxiety and stress by improving one's self-image in a negative way. Individuals will excuse their self-failures by blaming others. As a health-care provider, Penny has often heard the excuse, "My wife is such a good cook. Who can lose weight with all that good food around?" Refusal to accept and own self-behaviors and blaming others is an example of projection. Another kind of projection is applying your own feelings or characteristics to another person. Examples of this are if someone who lies and steals says, "Well, everyone does it," or a mate who does not remain faithful says, "All men are cheaters." These projection statements provide an excuse, avoid personal responsibility, and accuse others of the exact behavior that they are considering or doing. Pointing fingers and blaming is direct evidence that there is a lack of values and virtue in the life of that individual, and it should be a red flag to you.

When you can come to an understanding of why you feel the way you do, you can move on to address these emotions and deal with them in a positive, constructive manner. This will allow you to also look beyond the emotions and help find the underlying stress or problem that is the root cause of your emotions. Once you have dealt with the underlying problem, you should notice that your stress is reduced and that your emotions have been calmed.

"Realize that the emotions you are feeling at this very moment are a gift, a guideline, a support system, a call to action. If you suppress your emotions and try to drive them out of your life, or if you magnify them and allow them to take over everything, then you're squandering one of life's most precious resources."
—Anthony Robbins, *Awaken the Giant Within, page 249*

Positive stress

Not all stress is unhealthy. In their book, *The Power of Full Engagement*, Jim Loehr and Tony Schwartz present the theory that periods of stress followed by relaxation (or recovery) are a way to exercise the brain, similar to exercising any other muscle in the body. Common athletic training regimens suggest resting muscles for twenty-four to forty-eight hours after a strenuous workout. The same appears to be true for the brain. Normal stress, even excess stress for a short period of time, can be beneficial in "exercising" the brain. Excess stress for a prolonged period of time can be detrimental and actually do more damage than good without regular periods of recovery. Recovery can come in many forms, from something as simple as short regular breaks during the workday to scheduled vacations where all work is left behind and you have the opportunity to relax and refresh your mind.

Summary

Humans are emotional beings who can and will suffer. Even death can occur if emotional caring or excessive damage to the emotional makeup happens to a person. We have introduced many coping mechanisms dealing with emotions. Any coping mechanism can be helpful or harmful. When a coping mechanism moves you through a stressful situation safely, it is considered helpful. Harmful coping response is seen when there is no recognition of the clear and present danger and a negative outcome occurs for the individual or the relationship. If negative coping continues, the individual keeps repeating the same negative responses over and over again.

All forms of coping or dealing with stress impact relationships and how we deal with ourselves and others. As humans we demonstrate many types of actions or self-comfort measures when dealing with stress. There are attempts to transform the negative stress into positive feelings or pleasure. We seek pleasure through touch, rhythm, and sound. That is why music, dancing, and exercise are so therapeutic and help to reduce stress in most individuals.

Seeking your soul mate can be stressful, or it can also be viewed as an adventure. Look for and create positive stress management skills in yourself and within your soul mate to reduce drama and conflict in a relationship. Positive stress management can be living a life that is mostly free of drama, possessing a sense of humor, and sharing emotions. Take care of your physical self through exercise and sufficient, sound sleep. Have your own individual dreams and goals as well as goals shared with your mate. Communicate your needs to each other and listen to each other.

Chapter 4

Open communication

Words spoken render a picture of what is contained in the heart. Each spoken and written word possesses a meaning that springs from an emotional and or spiritual basis. The Hebrew language is amazing in that every letter of the alphabet has a spiritual meaning. Combining these letters creates words with deep, intense meaning and spiritual power. While words in the English language may not carry the same deep, spiritual meaning as those in Hebrew, they do convey our deepest thoughts. That is why the words that are spoken reveal the heart of the individual. Communication is how you can discover the condition and type of heart someone has. You must decide at some point in your communication with an individual if he or she is a soul mate or just another date.

There are many kinds of relationships in your life. You have friends, coworkers, family members, and social acquaintances, but we are going to focus on dating and how to find that special communication with your soul mate or improve communication with your date.

Time is precious, and time spent in a bad relationship is time lost forever. Settling for a relationship that is less than that of a soul mate connection is shortchanging yourself and your mate.

What is communication with a soul mate like? There is nothing more enjoyable than to be able to communicate openly and clearly with your soul mate. This communication can be intense and intimately sweet, pulling two souls into one. It is honest, trusting, and open, without boundaries or agendas. Your conversations can transcend time. These are the conversations that last for hours but seem like only minutes. When you look at the clock, you are amazed at how much time has passed. These conversations can be deep and intense or very simple in nature, but it is amazing how much time you can spend together and yet find that it seems no time at all has passed. There is an old saying, "Time flies when you are having fun." Finding a soul mate and making this level of connection requires both parties to be willing to open their emotions, heart, and soul to each other. There is a caution that must be given here. To communicate at this level requires you to be totally open and vulnerable to each other. The emotional walls that we put up to protect ourselves must come down. There must be trust and willingness for communication to happen at this level with both individuals. There should be no walls or boundaries, or no places of the heart that are denied or withheld. It is powerful, and it is not all sweetness. Sharing a deep love and communicating it is beyond pleasure, but you also have the power to deeply hurt, injure, or even destroy each other if that power is used unwisely.

Communication is speaking our thoughts and feelings that are to be shared and understood by others. Ideas and thoughts that form without any filters or control before we express them can be dangerous and harmful to relationships. The ideas and feelings expressed through words without any filter are like a wild man swinging a sword in a crowded room. It is foolish, harmful, and destructive. The tongue is thought to be a two-edged sword and to have the ability to cut a soul in two. Your tongue possesses the power to kill, but it also has the power to heal and express love. The tongue spewing out words uncontrollably is just as dangerous as the wild swordsman in a room. Words spoken (positive or negative) have the power to impact all those who are within hearing range.

"From the same mouth come praise and cursing. My brothers, this should not be."—James 3:10, NIV

Christian values bring this out in forty-four Bible verses that address the power of the spoken word. We are cautioned to think before speaking and to understand that words have the ability to heal, promote love, hurt, or even kill a soul. Proverbs 5:4, Proverbs 12:18, and 1 Peter 3:10 are three of the prominent forty-four verses for you to read.

Communication with each other is at some time or another going to be difficult or fail, even with the best of communicators. In an extraordinary relationship, you should not fear the possibility of miscommunication and being hurt, but accept the probability of it. It is never intended, but from time to time it will happen because we, as humans, are imperfect. There has never been recorded in all of history a relationship that has not had some form of challenge or hurt associated with love. When challenges of life and conflict arise, communicate with love. Strive to develop amazing communication that is shared, and seek to forgive and renew your love when miscommunication occurs. Do not let a situation of poor communication go for any length of time without resolution. Miscommunication unresolved begins to rot a relationship from the inside out.

Communication happens across all Four Relationship Cornerstones: intellectual, emotional, physical, and spiritual. Communication is how we express ourselves, make our needs known, and draw closer to others. Relationships at work, home, or in love all use the same principles of communication, but with love, dating, and the search for your soul mate, there is emotional, spiritual, and physical involvement that complicates communication. In this chapter we will approach both verbal and nonverbal forms of communication, such as body language and physical touch.

Verbal communication

The first and probably most common form of communication is verbal, with the less obvious component of verbal communication being listening. Open, honest communication is one of the greatest assets to a relationship. It is the free expression of our thoughts and feelings in a safe environment. Without this safety, openness, and expression, a relationship will suffer greatly and be mediocre at best. Extraordinary communication requires honest self-evaluation, honest evaluation of your partner, and an understanding of the communication abilities that exist between you. This form of communication requires both of you to be fearless, open to hurt, and vulnerable to each other. Communication is the vehicle that carries love, joy, pain, and sorrow. Excellent verbal communication can transmit your values, feelings, and ideas quickly and effectively. The end result is that the listener hears and translates the words, written or spoken, into understanding and feelings. When communication is lacking, ineffective, or poor, the result can be hurt, loneliness, and feelings of isolation or frustration. There is so much information already available about good communication and its importance to any relationship, yet most of us fail to take advantage of it. In most of the information we have read over the years, communication is the key missing component in most struggling or failed interpersonal relationships. We have verified this over and over in research by asking those soul mate couples who are together for many years, "To what do you attribute your being able to stay together all these years?" Communication is listed first or closely follows respect or shared giving.

Dating and getting to know someone immediately begins to test the communication patterns between the two of you. This should be thought of as an adventure. Men pursue beginning re-lationships with an excitement of paying attention to, chasing, and winning the woman's affections. Women love to be wooed and men love the chase. Early in relationships, communication is profuse through texting, phone calls, and special dates. Once the communication patterns are discovered and feelings are un-derstood, there is a slowing of intensity and time spent on com-municating. In mediocre relationships, men tend to lose interest, or their "hearing," after the infatuation is over. This is not so with your soul mate. The excitement continues, and you are willing to continue to work on perfecting the art of communication with your soul mate. Time spent away from your soul mate leaves you with a feeling of loss, and there is a desire to seek out his or her ideas, values, and comfort on even the very small day-to-day things. Great joy and comfort are found in sharing the small ev-eryday things of life.

Everyone communicates differently based on differences in emotional, spiritual, and intellectual openness. There are different styles of communication, and the key is to understand how you are communicating and to develop great communication skills. Soul mates connect and communicate in the same basic fashion. Finding someone who communicates effectively and who understands and appreciates your communication style is the key to an extraordinary relationship. All communication requires a sender and a receiver. Refer back to "Emotional maturity subcomponents, Dealing with re-ality constructively," in chapter 3.

Rick usually sends or delivers communications in direct and to-the-point fashion. He sometimes needs to pause before he speaks, being cautious to choose his words carefully. This is important, because his words can come across as harsh and uncaring, which is usually not the case. If his words come across as harsh and uncaring, his thoughts, ideas, or insight can very easily be lost on the listener because he or she could be feeling hurt, attacked, or disrespected. Penny struggles with how to send messages and being able to flip the communication switch from professional to personal. This has created difficulties in communication for her at times. As a professional health-care provider, she is trained to deliver communication based on what she thinks the receiver is asking for: direct and to the point, detailed with lots of information, or simple and uncomplicated. She is trained to filter out her emotions and feelings in delivering a response. This training includes not interjecting her feelings or emotions into situations, but to assist patients or manage crisis situations with critical thinking. It is a must that the communication styles flip on and off from professional to personal. On a personal level, she learned to acknowledge that she is free to share her emotions, thoughts, and ideas openly without reservation and struggle. It is a conscious decision to turn off the professional communication style in a personal relationship. When she became aware that she was responding as a professional within personal relationships, it was a challenge to step out of the safety and control that professional communication affords. It is difficult and scary for her to expose herself and become vulnerable on a personal level. It has taken an honest evaluation to come to this understanding, to give herself permission, and to acknowledge where she is and that it's OK to be there. Acknowledging her personal self-awareness has allowed her to open doors to emotional connections that were closed because of her training and her ease and comfort with control.

There are documented communication styles and differences between men and women. Women tend to communicate with a lot of words and ideas that pull from multiple areas of the brain at one time; most men...not so much. Men tend to communicate and discuss one issue from one area of the brain at one time, and this often creates confusion in communication when women are coming from a different point of reference. There is a documented and biological reason for this. The corpus callosum is the connection between the two hemispheres of the brain. This allows communication between both the right and left side of the brain at the same time. When the testosterone begins to be secreted in a male's body during development in the uterus, this connection becomes "burned" and becomes a one-lane highway going one direction. Females are not subject to the massive influence of testosterone, and the connection remains a six-lane interstate traveling both directions at the same time. The problem that is created in communication is that during conversation, women will pull information from both sides of the brain at once and change lanes so fast that the male is left wondering, "What in the world are you talking about? How did you get there from here?" This creates confusion and frustration for men if women don't slow down and explain or make it a point to stick to the singular topic and travel with the man in the same direction. An example of this is the woman starting a story in mid thought and leaving the man with no clue of what she is talking about. She then needs to be reminded to go back to the beginning of her story and fill in the details so that the man can catch up. For men, it requires them to have patience to listen to what may seem like too much information and take the time to process and sort through all the information coming at them like water out of a fire hose. Time and practice make communication effortless. You will find that there are some individuals who require much more effort to communicate with than others. Deborah Tannen has outlined some basic differences between male and female communications. Some of them are listed in the following table:

<u>**Men**</u>	<u>**Women**</u>
• Orient toward action	• Talk about it
• Solve problems	• Just listen
• Achieve results	• Focus on feelings and relationships
• Feel needed	• Feel cherished
• Feel appreciated and admired	• Feel respect and devotion
• Withdraw from stress	• Talk about stress
• Orient toward a goal	• Orient toward the relationship
• Offer advice	• Seek connection and understanding
• Transmit information	• Maintain interaction

Tannen, Deborah. 1990. *You Just Don't Understand: Women and Men in Conversation.* New York: Ballantine Books.

Whatever your style of communication, the basis of an extraordinary relationship is the ability to speak openly and freely with your mate about virtually any subject. If you find that this is lacking or there are communication blocks with your partner, this can be an indication of emotional upset, fear, lack of security, a misconnection, or inability to shift communication gears from professional to personal. It can also be an indication that you are not soul mates and there is not an extraordinary connection. This can be a huge red flag, and you need to seriously evaluate the situation and potentially terminate the relationship if extraordinary communication cannot be established.

We believe positive, healthy communication is one of the most critical aspects of an extraordinary relationship. The sender must be able to send messages, and, more importantly, the receiver must be willing to receive and hear the message. If you cannot communicate with each other, feelings, ideas, and concerns are not addressed properly or may never be addressed at all. The relationship begins to decay, and feelings of unhappiness and discontent begin to set in. We cannot emphasize this point enough, and men are typically not good at being in touch with emotions or the expression of them. The story of Adam and Eve is an example of a lack of being in touch with emotions and expression through communication. Adam was given responsibility and charge over the earth and naming all the animals. He found himself alone, and God created woman to be his companion and helper. God told them that they were able to eat of every fruit in the garden, except one. They understood that if they were to eat of the fruit on that tree, they would die. The story goes on to tell how Eve was convinced to partake of the fruit and did not die immediately, but became wise and came to know good from evil. She in turn shared this with Adam. They both knowingly had partaken in rebellion by not following God's command. It is interesting to note that when confronted by God, Adam blamed Eve, and Eve blamed the serpent. Neither Adam nor Eve accepted responsibility or accountability for their actions or personal choices. Instead they blamed someone other than themselves for their actions and flawed judgment. Extraordinary communication in a relationship means being accountable and owning your thoughts and actions. It also requires responsibility for the outcomes of what and how you communicate. Extraordinary relationships share those thoughts, ideas, and actions with self-ownership. Ownership is being accountable and responsible to each other and not blaming the other or someone else. It is this level of communication that brings challenges to relationships daily. Forgiveness, openness, loving, giving, and growing together (or apart) are choices that are made in even the very best of relationships.

Today we have many methods to communicate verbally: by phone, in person, by e-mail, or by text. We all know how to communicate, some more effectively and eloquently than others. But are we communicating or speaking from the heart and sharing our deepest thoughts, desires, and emotions? Or are we speaking just superficially? There is a significant difference, and the depth of communication you have with your mate will have a huge impact on the success of your relationship when both individuals are able and willing to open their emotions, thoughts, and desires to each other. To share these deep thoughts, desires, and emotions, you must understand who you are and what is important to you and be vulnerable enough to share those thoughts and feelings.

Some people have significant problems with communicating their ideas and feelings. Again, it tends to be men, but not always. Some people are just not able to verbalize their feelings until there is some triggering event, such as a comment or incident, and then, all of a sudden, ideas and feelings that may have been building for days or even weeks can come exploding out much like an erupting volcano. This type of communication can be extremely difficult to deal with unless you are very patient and understanding. It can also be dangerous because uncontrolled, hurtful, hateful words can be spoken, and they can never be taken back.

Words have meaning

In the English language, words can have multiple meanings. Choose your words wisely, because the message being sent may not be the one being received. For example, the saying "That was one hot dish" has several meanings. It could mean "That is one sexy woman" or "The food served was very hot and spicy." It takes more than one sentence to communicate the intent and meaning. Messages sent verbally are often taken differently than those sent by e-mail or text. E-mail and texting are flat forms of communication and are subject to the receiver reading in or out emotions that might or might not exist or be intended as part of the communication. Verbal communication has voice inflection to bring a deeper meaning to the message from the heart. You can hear this in person or on a phone conversation, but not in a text or e-mail. Attempts to convey emotions in electronic forms of communications have resulted in emoticons. You know them as smiley, frowny, tongue-sticking-out faces, and these are poor substitutes for actual emotions. It has been said that as much as 80 percent of the context of a message can be lost in an e-mail or text message because of the missing components of tone, inflection, and facial expression.

Rick was on a second or third date with a woman, and during their conversation she made a statement about an upcoming dog training event that she was planning on attending. As she described the event, she said, "You will see how great these dogs are and how much they have learned." In the context of that conversation, she was projecting a picture of the time when they would be together at an event that was very important to her. It indicated that she had interest in sharing something of importance to her. In a following conversation, she spoke in terms of "if." "If we spend time together," "If we are together," "If we attend this event together" all indicate that there is uncertainty about the future. While observations like these are not absolute and foolproof, they can be an excellent indicator of how a person perceives a situation or a relationship. As we said earlier, words have meaning. These conversations gave mixed signals as to what this woman was thinking and what she was looking for in a relationship with Rick. Whenever you think you are getting mixed signals, the best thing to do is to come right out and ask. As it turned out, some serious communication issues existed, and the relationship quickly ended.

To the astute observer, one can learn a significant amount about a speaker through the words they use. It is often said that words will betray a man's heart. The words that are chosen and how those words are used can give you great insight into what a person is thinking and what is in their heart. Remarks like "I'll bet you say that to all the guys" or "I'll bet you just love 'em and leave 'em" are typically remarks that show insecurity, especially if they are directed to the same person several times. It is a roundabout way for the speaker to see if you have sincere interest, are looking for a one-night stand, or are just stringing them along for personal gain.

Ways to communicate

Communication today is full of options that were never available to the masses in the past. Historically communication would be letters or face-to-face conversation. The various forms of communication today include Skype, video chats, phone calls, texting, e-mails, letters, or prerecorded messages on DVDs or MP3 files. You may have people seeking relationships from a distance or across the room with these options. We have seen couples sitting in a restaurant; both have their eyes cast down onto their cell phones, missing quality time together. One or both may be answering the phone, creating interruptions and distractions with incoming texts, calls, e-mails, or tweets. Many communication options will be present as you meet people and date. Verbal communication that is in person affords you the opportunity to see the facial and body language that comprise more of what is being said than the words alone. It is easier for communication errors to occur outside of face-to-face interaction. Feelings, emotions, and thoughts cannot easily hide from face-to-face communication. The face, body, and eyes will give you clues to what the heart and mind are really thinking and feeling. Learning how to read and understand the meaning that people intend can add to success in all relationships—work, dating, family, and friends.

Express your feelings

Emotions bring feelings to communication, and that can bring special challenges. If you are the type of person who has difficulty expressing your feelings or concerns, take an inward look at yourself and try to figure out what holds you back. Understanding what holds you back is the first step in figuring out how to communicate more effectively with your mate. For some people, getting professional help to deal with significant personal issues may be advisable. Learning to express your feelings in a respectful, open, and honest way will help you create a significantly stronger connection with your mate.

Men, this is where we tend to stumble and fall. Most of us were taught that if we showed any emotions other than negative emotions, such as anger or frustration, we were wimps. If we showed any positive emotions, such as love or tenderness, or even cried, we would be considered sissies. As we have discussed previously, God gave us emotions for a reason. It is ultimately not healthy to turn our emotions inward and withhold them from your mate. Being able to share our emotions with our mate is an incredibly important part of the communication process and the future success of our relationship. If we keep our emotions closed off from our mate, we put distance between the two of us. In essence we are building a wall that our mate will have difficulty climbing over, going around, or breaking through. Time and again, studies have shown that communicating feelings frees the body and mind of stress, which, in turn, creates a healthier you both physically and mentally.

"The walls we build around us to keep out the sadness also keep out the joy."—Jim Rohn

Successful communication of emotions will bring healthy benefits to the relationship that are physical and psychological. We have found that one of the unique aspects of communicating with your soul mate verbally is the calming effect of your mate's voice. Just hearing their voice, whether it is in person or on the phone, has a wonderful calming effect. If you are having a really stressful day, just a couple of minutes of phone time can have a significant physiological effect that removes much of your stress and seems to make everything right with the world. Communicating with your loved one gives you the chance to draw closer together.

Excellent communication and expression of emotions can be learned. It may not be easy, but it is possible. In Penny's case, she had to become brave enough to let her true thoughts and feelings be known. It is, many times, a matter of stepping outside your comfort zone. The great thing is that once you have expressed yourself in an uncomfortable situation, it usually becomes easier the next time you are in a difficult or uncomfortable situation. Emotional awareness helps you to:

- Understand and empathize with others.

- Understand yourself and what you want.

- Stay motivated in a relationship even though you might not like someone's message.

- Communicate hard messages clearly and effectively and build strong, trusting relationships that are able to work creatively together.

- Solve problems and resolve conflicts.

When you know how to do this, you can remain in control of your emotions and behavior, even in very challenging situations, and communicate more clearly and effectively.

Listening

Another component of communication is listening. Listening shares many of the same characteristics with speaking. Are you allowing others, especially your significant other, to share their deepest thoughts, desires, and emotions? Are you truly listening, or are you more focused on your response? Effective listening will make the speaker feel heard and understood which can help build a stronger, deeper connection between you. Listening is an art that can be learned. It takes practice to listen to what the speaker says, ask the speaker open-ended questions, and then allow him or her to answer without interruption. After listening, repeat back what you understood him or her to say. You can improve the depth of your relationship through communications by helping clarify information, which will help avoid conflicts and misunderstandings. If the speaker agrees that you have heard them correctly, you may proceed to ask additional questions to get a greater depth of understanding until you are both confident that you fully understand each other. This does not necessarily mean that you will agree. It simply means that you understand each other.

Listening effectively is important to relieve negative emotions. When emotions are running high, listening effectively can be calming, relieve negative feelings, and allow for real understanding or problem solving to begin when the speaker feels that he or she has been truly heard. Reaffirm what they have told you and then recap their thoughts as you understand them. You may also want to ask if there is anything they need from you or anything you can do for them if it is appropriate. Create an environment where everyone feels safe to express ideas, opinions, and feelings or can plan and problem solve in creative ways. This will create a significant bond with your mate, and they will feel much closer and more connected to you. This is not a trick, scheme, or tactic to be emotionally or intellectually at-tractive to someone. It is a legitimate communication technique. As Stephen Covey said in his book *The Seven Habits of Highly Effective People*, "Seek first to understand and then be understood."

Tips for effective listening

- Focus fully on your mate.

- Avoid interrupting.

- Avoid seeming judgmental.

- Show your interest.

If your goal is to fully understand and connect with another per-son, listen effectively. The more you practice, the more connected and rewarding your interactions with others will become.

Prayer

One of the greatest forms of communication is prayer. While this may not be direct communication with your mate, it *is* direct communication with God. God intercedes for us in most situations if it is His will. We encourage you to pray about any relationship you are seeking or are in. He will guide you...if you listen. God knows what is on your heart, so just ask for what you are seeking. If it is something or someone that He wants you to have, then He will bring that thing or person into your life. He doesn't necessarily go *poof* and what you want automatically appears. He will guide you and show you what you need to do to achieve what you are seeking. Many times, if not most times, it will seem that He is making you wait for what you seek. Is it that He makes us wait, or are we expecting God to deliver our heart's desire on our time schedule? He wants us to have patience, something that very few of us have these days since we live in a world of instant gratification. He may also have lessons that need to be learned before we move on or are given our heart's desires.

Seeking your soul mate is no different than seeking any other worldly possession. God always wants what is best for us. An extraordinary relationship is no different. We need to be patient, wait on His timing, and learn the lessons He wants us to learn before we can move into an extraordinary relationship. If we try to proceed without His blessing and without learning the specific lessons He needs us to learn, I can almost guarantee you that your relationship will not be extraordinary and will more than likely fail. Even if you find the person you believe to be your soul mate, if God does not sanction the relationship, it will be less than extraordinary. Praying together as a couple for God's will is more powerful than a single prayer offered up. As the two of you pray and listen to hear God's direction for your lives individually and together, miracles happen and the power of God is revealed.

In the end, communicate your wishes (pray) to God. He is listening. Just because He does not give you the answer *you* are looking for or on your time line doesn't mean that His answer is no. It may just mean that He has something even better in mind for you.

Remain patient and open to possibilities that you cannot begin to comprehend.

Values

Communication is based on the personal values that we hold. The social ideals that mean the most to you are called your values. Values that are foundational to extraordinary communication are respect, honesty, openness, safety, and shared giving.

Respect

Respect, vt.: to honor; to have consideration for. Respect is an important part of communication. It is something that is earned and is given freely. It cannot be demanded. You need to earn the respect of your mate and give him or her the respect they deserve and the respect that you would like to receive. It is giving your mate uninterrupted and undivided attention when they are speaking. It is allowing them to have their opinion even if you disagree, and working together to find a solution to the issues at hand.

Respectful communication is any type of communication that is kind and courteous. It begins with good manners and a careful choice of words. To communicate proper respect, you need to meet and greet an individual with proper etiquette for the situation. Different social settings require different interactions, and using proper etiquette will help avoid offensive communication. Respectful communication will refrain from quick, impulsive, lengthy, emotionally charged statements that are spoken or written. Kind tones of voice indicate a civility and lack of judgmentalism and are less likely to be misinterpreted as attacking. This improves your chance of being understood fully. Graciousness and a mature nature are conveyed when you confirm, empathize, and sympathize as you listen. Speaking honestly and kindly and offering constructive, helpful words and thoughts are foundational to respectful communication.

Have you ever received a long e-mail or phone call that went on and on from a person you really did not want to communicate with? We all have had unwanted visitors drop in and wondered if they were ever going to leave. Respect is demonstrated by not sending unwanted e-mails or phone calls or pursuing a relationship that is unwanted. Conversing with people respectfully is honoring their time, not to exaggerate or oversimplify the message. Speak freely but not in a childlike fashion to another adult. Do not believe hearsay or information that is overheard by a third party. This kind of information and communication is gossip and is unfounded. It can be very hurtful and destructive to your relationship. Believing a third-party communication is disrespectful and does not allow the person in question an opportunity to share the truth. It devalues the person you are speaking with.

When dealing with a relationship, follow up a written form of communication with a phone call or a personal visit. This allows you the opportunity to validate that your written message was received and understood correctly. Any misinterpretations can be quickly corrected.

True, honest, kind smiles go a long way toward being respectful and caring in communication, and they convey acceptance. Being a good listener and putting aside your own agenda indicates a deep respect. It is respectful to offer support, but not solve the issues discussed.

Respectful Communication Guidelines

R—Accept *responsibility* for what you say and feel without blaming others.

E—Listen with an *energized* heart.

S—Be *sensitive* to differences in communication styles.

P—*Ponder* on what you hear and feel before you speak.

E—*Examine* your own assumptions and perceptions.

C—Keep *confidentiality*.

T—*Trust* ambiguity, because we are not here to debate who is right or wrong.

Adapted from the Respectful Communication Guidelines, Kaleidoscope Institute. First printed in The Bush was Blazing but Not Consumed by Eric H. F. Law.

Communicating with respect involves conversations using 'I' statements. This means owning your feelings by stating your thoughts, needs, and feelings in whole statements. An example would be, "I really feel bad when you _____ ." Fill in the blank with the behavior that is upsetting. When you clearly state your thoughts with respect, your soul mate should respond by listening and reaffirming your concern. A healthy conversation should ensue.

Compare the "*I*" statement with a disrespectful "*You*" statement: "You are disgusting when you always _____." The "*You*" statement is judgmental and attacking. It will place your soul mate on the defensive and is not respectful communication. It is not clear to your partner what your real issues are when you use "*you*" statements because your partner feels they are under attack. You need to clearly define and express your concerns or feelings through "*I*" statements. Great communication is not creating conversations that blame, attack, and drag out old history or make negative comparisons. Respectful and wise communication is foundational to successful relationships.

Honesty

Without a doubt, the one crucial element of extraordinary communication is honesty. Without honesty, there can be no trust. Without trust you can have nothing more than an arm's-length relationship. The best way to build trust is to always tell the truth. You have to feel free to be honest, both with your mate and with yourself.

> *"If you tell the truth, you don't have to remember anything."*
> —*Mark Twain*

How do you become honest with yourself? You have to do a realistic self-evaluation about your emotions, abilities, desires, and passions. To develop an extraordinary relationship, you must be honest right from the start about your feelings and emotions, your wants and desires, and your abilities and disabilities. Everything should be out on the table. Does this all need to be done on the first date? No, but you should cover these topics and any others that are important to you in the first few dates. You should be learning about the key aspects of a person early on before too many emotions become involved. If you have something to hide, you're probably not a good candidate for an extraordinary relationship.

> *"Whoever can be trusted with very little can also be trusted with much, and whoever is dishonest with very little will also be dishonest with much."*—*Luke 16:10*

For whatever reason, most guys don't seem to grasp the concept of honesty when it comes to dating. Both Penny and I have heard horror stories about men, especially on dating websites, who lie about body type, alcohol/drug use, looks, and interests, among other things. When dishonesty is involved and you meet your date for the first time in person, it is a total disappointment. Sometimes the disappointment is so great that the date ends immediately after introductions because you were totally misled. People are notorious for lying about their age and posting photos of themselves from ten, fifteen, or even twenty years ago.

Trust is something that every relationship must have. Trust must be earned, and if it is lost, it may never be gained back. Honesty spawns trust. Your mate can be trustworthy in most areas of his or her life but may have some personal flaws that they try to hide or cover up. If they are willing to lie about a small personal character flaw, what else might they be willing to lie about? These lies can be very simple, such as posting a ten-year-old picture on a dating website. Is it a picture of you? Yes, it is. Is it an honest representation of what you look like today? No, it is not. One of the most common lies that is told, and it seems to be socially acceptable, is about age. For some reason in our society it is impolite to ask a woman her age. In the real world of dating, it can be a significant issue, especially if the lie hides a significant age discrepancy.

You may be in a relationship in which you have a great connection in two or three of the Four Relationship Cornerstones. However, deception destroys honesty. For example, if your mate hides other relationships from you when you have agreed to be monogamous, you will lose any basis for trust if you discover one or more additional relationships.

Deceptions may be hard to detect at times. If you have a mate who deceives about his or her emotions and feelings, it may be difficult to determine the truth. An example to illustrate this is to be dating someone who does not clearly understand and thus cannot be truthful about their feelings. As discussed earlier in this book, some people are not emotionally mature because of their past and how they learned to cope in a dysfunctional family. That dysfunction hindered their ability to be honest with themselves about their feelings, and consequently they cannot be honest with you. Dishonesty and dysfunction are signs of a toxic relationship and need to be avoided. You deserve to have the most extraordinary relationship possible.

Openness

You have to have open communications with your mate. This means that you can talk about any subject without fear of reprisal. Depending on how you were raised, common subjects that can be difficult for many adults to talk about are finances, sex, politics, and religion. Many of us were raised in households where these subjects were taboo. They were just topics that you didn't discuss, especially outside the home. A stigma was created that there is something wrong with talking openly about sometimes difficult topics.

Another aspect of being open with your mate is that you don't hide information from them. For example, if you are having financial difficulty or have run up large credit card bills, your mate has no way of helping, much less understanding some of the pressures or stress you are having, if you don't share with your mate about the debt. Talking about sex can be embarrassing for some people. Most of the time there is embarrassment because they have never had any real conversations about the subject with a member of the opposite sex. These types of conversations are important to have *before* marriage or a committed, long-term relationship because any red flags or incompatibility issues can be discussed and worked out before too much time is invested in a wrong relationship.

Openness must go in both directions. If one person is open and the other is not, only one half of the connection is being made and extraordinary communication does not exist. Even if the subjects are difficult or sensitive, they must be on the table for discussion.

Safety

Feeling safe in a conversation is important for open, honest communication. If you or your mate does not feel safe to communicate your deepest thoughts or feelings, you cannot connect at the most intimate and important level. You both need to be able to communicate your most intimate desires, needs, and feelings without fear. Yes, some of these subjects may be difficult to discuss, especially the first time or two that you talk about them. However, the more of these conversations you have, the easier they become. If your mate is expressing his or her deepest feelings, do not negate or marginalize them. Do not use anything they share with you to attack, belittle, or demean your mate. Do not share these personal feelings with anyone else without permission, especially if they will be embarrassing to your mate. These are excellent ways to get your mate to shut down and not share anything deeply personal with you. You have to understand that your mate is trying to share information with you that they feel is very important to your relationship. This is information that you need in order to gain a much deeper understanding of your mate. The more you know about your mate, the more you can connect in the Four Cornerstones of a Relationship. The key here is to help your mate feel safe to talk to you and to use any information shared in a positive, constructive way.

Negative or abusive talk is not to be tolerated. It causes harm to those against whom it is directed and can also harm all who are in listening range. We have discussed earlier that words have meaning and hold the power to build up or tear down. This power extends to all who hear your conversations.

A young man shared with Penny that he heard his parents fighting and felt like he wanted to go hide from the pain he felt from hearing the argument. He watched them argue and saw that the words they spoke were like arrows. These arrows flew in all directions to all those who were within listening distance. He saw how the negative words were poison-tipped arrows causing injury to those who heard the words even though they were not the intended target. As the argument subsided and kinder words were spoken, he saw that these kinder words were also like arrows that delivered a warm, fuzzy, happy, loving feeling when they hit. He understood at an early age that words have meaning and impact all those within hearing range in a negative or positive way.

It is important that you do not subject yourself to negative, angry conversations. While they will happen from time to time, these conversations do not produce positive outcomes. Conversations need to be held without anger and negativity. Excuse yourself from a negative conversation to diffuse the situation. After a cool down period, make it a point to follow up in writing or with a phone call. Test the waters to make sure it is safe to have a calm, positive discussion. Allow yourself to be respectful in your conversation, and insist on the same respectful treatment. Respect is something that will return to you when you give it. You deserve respect and must give respect when it is earned. If negative or hurtful conversations become a regular way of communicating, red flags should be popping up and you should be reevaluating your relationship and whether it should continue.

Shared giving

When we interviewed couples and asked, "To what do you attribute your success or the length of your relationship?" we discovered that their longevity was due to their ability to give unconditionally to their relationship throughout the years. Giving unconditionally includes or means that there are no expectations or counting tit for tat. Often they expressed that their relationship is not 50/50 but giving 110 percent and not expecting anything in return. It was expressed by one couple that taking the time to listen and hold your tongue when you really don't feel like listening was a gift of shared giving. Another example of shared giving would be to give space and time to your loved one when what you really want is to talk and understand. These are but two examples. Your giving may take very different forms.

Chapter 5

Nonverbal communication

Communication is so much more than words. Studies have shown that 60 percent of communication is nonverbal. A simple touch or look from your soul mate or someone you love deeply can bring peace and harmony to chaos. There is so much that is said in facial expressions, the tone of voice, body language, silence, and even the physical distance between individuals. We discussed the various components for excellent verbal communication, and in this section we will look at the components that make up excellent nonverbal communication.

Distance

Distance in the context of this discussion is considered to be the space between individuals measured in feet as opposed to miles. Distance speaks to how open or social the relationship is, or the relationship intent of the individual. Understanding and interpreting distance helps you to read the intent of someone you do not know well. When I (Penny) go on a first date, I have already screened the man and the date is for getting to know this individual better. First dates always create some nervous tension. When meeting a person for the first time, if your date breaks the two-foot barrier with a hug or touch, that means they are attracted to you. If the person keeps their distance without touch, it might be that they are insecure or thinks the relationship doesn't have potential. Or it might mean that physical touch is not one of their primary love languages. You need to understand that this is not a reflection on you as a person, but a reflection of their feelings.

With a first meeting, I (Penny) do just fine when there is a table between us or some other physical barrier. When there are no physical barriers, I become uncomfortable with close proximity if a person violates the two-foot zone and stays there. This uncomfortable feeling intensifies when I do not feel a strong attraction to the person. By quickly moving away to extend the space between us, I have come to understand that I am sending a message of non intimate interest. Here is a general guide to the interpretation of the distance between two people.

Intimate distance (touching to one-and-a-half feet): This is the distance of kissing, lovemaking, wrestling, comforting, and protecting.

Personal distance (one-and-a-half feet to four feet): This distance is a no-contact distance, and it is reserved for people who are more than just casual friends or acquaintances. Inviting a person within this close circle indicates a deeper interest and relationship. This proximity causes conflict in a relationship if a person of the opposite sex is invited in when your significant other is near. Close friendships of the same sex are not viewed as an intrusion or threat to opposite-sex relationships.

Social distance (four to twelve feet): Impersonal business or casual conversations are experienced in this space. This space is not viewed as a threat and is acceptable in getting to know or work with someone.

Public distance (twelve to twenty-five feet or farther): This distance is outside the circle of friendship or work relationships and is for all public occasions.

We all have our comfort zone or "bubble" around us. It is living, dynamic, and ever changing as people enter our presence, or our emotional attachments and feelings change. So how do you learn and improve your nonverbal communication? Practice! Go out and "people watch" in large public settings. Watch for nonverbal communication and notice how others react to it. Try to guess the relationship between them. Become more aware of cultural, religious, and gender differences. Look for grouping or clusters of nonverbal communications to get a better picture of what is communicated. When you are in a group or personal setting, you should use words that support your nonverbal actions. Do not let your body contradict what your words are saying. Videotape yourself and listen to how you sound and the tone of your voice when speaking. Look objectively at your body language (which we will discuss shortly) and facial expressions and listen to your tone of voice to make sure you are conveying a uniform message.

Paralanguage and silence

Tucked within nonverbal communication is paralanguage. It consists of silence, voice inflection, and tone. Have you heard it said, "It's not what you say, but how you say it"? Paralanguage is the study of voice inflection and communication. "Wow! That was a good meal" could be spoken with the intent of being a compliment or a direct insult, depending on how it is vocalized. Communicating through e-mail and text as a primary source of getting to know someone is nearly impossible when you want to fully understand the intent of the conversation, because so much is lost without intonation and inflection. In close relationships texts and e-mails can be supplemented with inflection because of the knowledge of the sense of humor, intellect, or emotional state of the individual. You can't hear anger, love, passion, kindness, and emotions delivered through a text or e-mail; you can only assume or presume to understand.

The absence of any communication is itself making a comment. In verbal or written communication, to skip over or avoid a subject is a red flag and requires more investigation. Do not drop the ball here. Silence is powerful and may be an indicator of not feeling safe to communicate thoughts and feelings, or it may be a closed emotional door. You need to ask yourself, if the subject matter is not open for discussion, then why is that door closed? Is it anger, fear, lying, hiding, or asking too soon for too much personal information? There are occasions where silence is an indication of not being sure or able to communicate, and it is appropriate to allow and accept this. Some of the best communication occurs through holding someone closely and not speaking a word.

Look for the nonverbal communication tucked within the spoken message. Listen to the tone of voice and inflection. Observe body language, distance between you, touch, and other senses to improve communication accuracy for sending as well as receiving the message that is intended.

Body language

Body language can be a very important part of communication and is the best known type of nonverbal communication. Reading body gestures is the art and pastime of people watchers. How people stand or how they are seated can reveal a lot about whether they are interested or uninterested in the conversation. Are they facing you directly? Are they standing at an angle to you? Are they making direct eye contact? Are their arms folded across their chest, or are they relaxed down at their sides? If you are seated, is the other person leaning into you or away from you? Are their legs crossed or hands clasped? While you might not realize it, all of these positions may have meaning in your conversation and will let you know if the person you are with is interested in your conversation or not. A person facing toward you, toes or feet pointed toward you, and looking you in the eye conveys interest. A person with arms and legs uncrossed, sitting up, leaning inward toward and facing you demonstrates openness to your conversation and the relationship. A semi reclined position, legs open and arms at the side, expresses real comfort. Crossed arms or legs, hanging a leg over the arm of a chair, or straddling a chair backward with arms crossed expresses indifference or a closed attitude. Another sign of indifference or a closed attitude is when the newspaper, TV, phone, or another preoccupation with your surroundings distracts someone when you are attempting to communicate with them verbally. Being aware of and learning to read body language will help you understand the true intent of the individual and his or her communication.

Having had the privilege of being in sales for most of my adult life I (Rick) have come to notice and appreciate some of the subtle differences of body language and facial expression. Facial expression is one of the easiest aspects of body language for me to read. We should all be able to recognize the more dramatic facial expressions of a smile, look of surprise, or frown. If facial features start to tense up, such as a slight lowering of the eyebrows and slight downturn of the corners of the mouth, stress, sadness, or frustration may be present. On the other hand, raised eyebrows and a slight upturn in the corner of the mouth can indicate happiness, pleasure, or satisfaction. I (Penny) have discovered that smiles can hold a wide variety of meaning, and it is not always happiness. The oblong smile is when you smile politely in a grimace with lips drawn tight and thin. As an example, this smile is used to shake off too much attention from a drunken person's comment or off-color joke that you do not appreciate. A simple smile is one you typically have when you are by yourself when you hear or see something amusing or loving. The upper smile has upper teeth showing and is used with eye-to-eye contact to greet friends or parents. It is known as the "how-do-you-do smile." A broad smile is one of pleasurable excitement that has full teeth, upper and lower, showing. The mouth is open and lips are curled back.

How do you know when you meet someone if they are interested in you? When someone is really interested, you will notice preening gestures. These are acts performed by either sex in an unconscious way. These gestures include standing tall, pulling in a potbelly, arranging clothing, straightening a tie, checking out fingernails, and pushing back or playing with hair. While someone is talking to you, you may see them check himself or herself out in a mirror or reflection of a window. They are making sure they are looking good for you. Preening and smiles are a great start with nonverbal body language, but there is more. Body language often happens in clusters to include distance, appearance, eye contact, facial expression, and touch. When a person is interested, you will see eye contact, his or her body facing you, an adjusting of clothing, and movement to reduce the distance that exists between you. Nonverbal flirting is very powerful when mastered and can also discourage quickly those you are not interested in. Breaking eye contact, turning your back to the individual, and keeping distance between you indicates disinterest.

Eyes

The first personal interaction you will likely have with an individual is eye contact. So much information is communicated within seconds that an opinion is formed and you have created a first impression. It is difficult, if not impossible, to change first impressions. Saint Augustine called the eyes "the window to the soul." When you learn how to look into the eyes and read them, you can see into a person's soul. Relationships of all types begin with the initial viewing of a person, and this triggers thoughts of either wanting to get to know them or not having any desire to know them at all.

What do the eyes tell us? How do you read eyes in a dating relationship? Eye contact begins with short glimpses and then looking away. Direct eye-to-eye contact for one to two seconds indicates interest. What can interrupt direct eye contact? Looking away is typical of trying to avoid unwanted contact with someone. When we feel shame or do not want our true feelings to be discovered, our instinct is to cover our eyes or turn away. When you experience this, it indicates that there is no interest or the person is uncomfortable. The depth of interest can be indicated by the length of eye contact. There are times when prolonged eye contact between a man and a woman may be construed as being overly intimate or intrusive. There is a time and a place for a prolonged gaze between a man and a woman. In a romantic relationship, it can convey intense emotion and passion and be very exciting.

There are many studies on the eyes and the importance of what is communicated through the eyes. Learning about the movement of the eye, pupil size, and reading the expression improves your ability to understand and communicate. You can practice beginning skills on yourself. Take the time to look into the mirror and notice the size of your pupils. Now think intently on something very pleasurable for a couple of minutes while watching your pupil size. What happens? Did they grow bigger? Of course they did! This is a normal response to pleasurable thoughts. If you notice your date looking intently at you during a conversation and the pupils enlarge, they are more than likely attracted to you. This type of communication cannot be hidden or covered up. It is always possible that your date is thinking of something other than you that is pleasurable and that causes the pupil dilation, but this is not likely if they are gazing directly at you without any other eye movement. The pupils can dilate for other reasons, including being in a darkened room or the use of drugs, among other things, so it is important to read other facial features and body language along with the eyes.

What does it mean when you notice eye movements that are up, down, side to side, or a combination of these? This movement will give you clues on how someone learns and listens. You can assess how a person learns, relates, and communicates from eye movement. Eye contact and eye movement are one avenue to extraordinary communication that can happen when there are two individuals communicating in the same style or learning pattern. There are three patterns or styles of learning: visual, auditory, and kinesthetic. Up-and-down eye movement indicates a visual style of learning and communication. You might hear the person make a statement such as "I like the way you look at things." Side-to-side or right-to-left eye movement indicates an auditory learning and communication style. A statement you might hear in the conversation is "Do you hear what I mean?" Lastly, eye movement downward and from side to side indicate the kinesthetic or feeling style of communication. When feelings are involved, the eyes will look down, and you might hear something like "Do you get the same feeling as I?" What does it mean when you see a combination eye movement? A combination movement of up and to the left indicates memory recall. Ask the question "What was the model of your first car?" and you will find eye movement up and to the left as the person recalls the memory. Eye movement up and to the right indicates a creation of thoughts and ideas. It is commonly thought that someone who is looking up and to the right is creating an answer or lying.

The eyes clearly show expressions of feelings, and this is an international language. There are seven universal emotions: anger, contempt, fear, disgust, happiness, sadness, and surprise. There are ten thousand facial expressions, and three thousand of them are relevant to emotion. Most people use fifty to sixty expressions in normal conversation. These expressions can last one to three seconds and are known as macro expressions, with most people being able to notice and read these expressions. There are micro expressions that last as little as one-twenty-fifth of a second that very few individuals are able to see and read. The expressions of the eyes that all can easily see include the following: An eyebrow furrowing and a narrowing of the eyes indicate anger. A raising of the eyebrows and eyes that are wide open indicate surprise. A twinkle and a softening of the muscles surrounding the eyes indicate love.

It is a common perception and studies have indicated that adults with large eyes tend to be viewed as more honest. Beady little eyes are thought to indicate dishonesty. Usually, people who are thought to have baby faces or more attractive faces are characterized by large eyes (and this can be cultural). Learning how to read the eyes will give you insight beyond words into the interest, emotions, and psychological state of the person you are around. Simple observations can help discern what a person's mood is or what they are thinking just by looking at or into their eyes.

The Seven Basic Emotions and their Universal Expressions

Anger

Fear

Surprise

Sadness

Disgust

Contempt

Joy

Humintell

(c) David Matsumoto 2011

Eye contact is an important part of communication right from the very beginning of the first contact with someone. Initial eye contact can signal interest, just as the lack of eye contact can signal no interest. Being single and searching for that special someone is an adventure, and meeting people for the first time has the mind asking, "Could this be the one?" Relationships travel through stages, and they begin with the eyes. There you are and you spot that hottie who catches your eye. This can happen anywhere and at any time. You see him or her and you feel that they are attractive. You glance in their direction and hope they notice you. Then it happens...your eyes meet. In this moment there is progression from the eye contact to body language with smiles and body posturing or looking away. Often discouragement settles in with singles at this point if you are interested and the other person looks away. It is a chance you take when you notice someone and they notice you. They open up or close down. Frustration can set in when eye contact is made but it goes no further. Know that this person is not available or may not be seeking a relationship. He or she may sincerely have no interest, they may be married or in a relationship, or may be homosexual, and it is no reflection on your worth as an individual. Your self-worth should not be determined or adversely impacted by their lack of interest.

To keep from being discouraged, focus on your Must Haves for your soul mate. The key is being patient. Having an open heart and mind with your eyes wide open is the beginning. Seek the truth and look for the best. You are worthy of the very best and should not settle for anything less than extraordinary. When someone is interested, there is openness to you, and this is indicated with a smile and progression to voice or touch contact. The initial contact that follows the eye contact is when there are accidental body bumps, handshakes, the famous one-liner openings are stated, or "Can I have this dance" occurs. This progression can take seconds to weeks, depending on the individuals, situations, and circumstances involved. This can be very time consuming, and your time is precious. Only you can decide how much time, if any, you want to spend in this kind of dating pattern.

Touch

The nonverbal communication of touch is often underrated and misunderstood. The skin is the largest organ in the body, and this organ is the first form of communication an infant understands. A loving touch, a touch in anger, or a lack of touch can cause an infant to thrive or close down and die. The lack of touch in a relationship is a challenge and has caused the death of many relationships. It is through the fingers that energy is communicated and speaks a language through touch. How does that happen? When you love and care for someone, each touch or caress shares energy and love. Caring and loving touch triggers biochemical changes within the brain that are thought to be a hormone named oxytocin, which will maintain or advance a relationship. Similarly, a lack of touch can destroy a relationship because of the limited hormone release in the brain. Touch is so very important to maintain a relationship, and a lack of touch will result in a slow death of something that was once beautiful.

Nonverbal touching is interpreted differently based on cultures. Opening doors, gentle guidance with a touch on the arm or back, or holding a hand to help guide someone up or down stairs as a form of protection can be a common courtesy or an expression of a desire for deeper intimacy. Hand holding and an arm around a shoulder are declarations of friendship or love. Hugs between friends or with someone you love are the form of touch least likely to be rebuffed. Within some cultures it is expected for social acquaintances to hug on meeting, and this can be awkward when cultures clash.

For a couple to have their arms around the waist of the other is a declaration and statement of amorous intimacy and a desire for deeper intimacy and other forms of intimate touch, such as kissing. Kissing is a very intimate expression of emotions, passion, and affection toward the person you are with. A simple kiss on the lips along with frontal hugs is borrowed from social norms of friends and family saying hello or farewell. The exchange of a kiss is an open expression of intimate desires without using words.

Progression from initial visual contact to intimate touch has been well documented. The visual contact is the beginning expression of interest, and as the relationship progresses it can move through stages from vision to touch. Touch is an intimate expression of caring and affection.

Touching and physical distances vary for different cultures. America is a melting pot of various cultures, and there can be great frustration and confusion due to the many different cultural views on touch. It is wise to understand cultural differences when in a relationship and how those views can and do impact your relationship. Here are a few examples of the differences between countries:

1. Minimal touch countries: Japan, United States, United Kingdom, and Australia.

2. Moderate touch countries: France, China, and India.

3. High touch countries: Middle East, Latin countries, and Italy.

You may be surprised at this list and where each country falls on the list. Contrary to popular belief, it is rare in the United States to meet and greet simple acquaintances with a handshake, a hug, or a kiss on the cheek. We will nod and say hello or smile and wave from a distance as a greeting. In other countries it is offensive not to stop, shake hands, hug, or offer a simple kiss on the cheek when greeting a simple acquaintance. Frequency of touch also varies significantly between different cultures. In 1978 a foundational study by R. G. Harper referred to several studies, one of which examined touching in coffee houses. During a one-hour sitting, researchers observed 180 touchings for Puerto Ricans, 110 for the French, none for the English and two for Americans. Touch is a powerful tool in communication and can be used to bring you closer together, or it can become a wedge to drive you apart. You can feel the power in touch, and it is accepted or rejected based on individual likes and strong cultural influences.

There are studies and theories that have taken touch to a new level. It has been studied to the extent that touch can be classified into five different categories or types of touch. So now there is a challenge to interpret what desires are behind the nonverbal communication of touch. The first touch is likely to be more accidental than premeditated; it involves touching a neutral body part. The recipient either accepts the touch or rejects it by moving away. Accidental touches are perceived as unintentional and have no meaning. They consist mainly of brushes or bumping into another person.

Touch in social settings is much more likely to communicate a desire to progress to an intimate relationship. Work touch and social touch are similar, with the exception that it is acceptable in social settings for touch to communicate desire for a deeper and more intimate relationship. So what is communicated through touch? Touch shows a concern or a desire to serve, nurture, reassure, promise, or protect. Drawing close and playful touches with mutual teasing express affection through poking, tickling, or startling. There is an emotional connection to touch in social settings that moves a relationship to a deeper, more intimate level than in the work setting.

In the workplace, you may experience a variety of different types of touch. They may include both appropriate and inappropriate touching. While we realize that there can be unwanted and inappropriate touch in the workplace, the negative aspects of this type of touch are not within the scope of this book. We simply want to make you aware that not all touch is sexual in nature. You may experience the touch of appreciation as an expression of gratitude for something you have done. Examples would be a handshake, safe hug, or a pat on the back. Just because you have been physically touched, it does not mean that there was intent or desire for deeper intimacy or a relationship. Nonsexual hugs or touches are brief (one to two seconds max), are on neutral, clothed body parts, and do not require full body contact. Contact that lasts longer can become uncomfortable and may be communicating undesired attention.

The workplace can be confusing if you feel an attraction toward a coworker. Workplace romances happen on a regular basis and can create a strained working environment not only for the couple but coworkers as well. There are corporate policies governing workplace romance to protect individuals from sexual harassment. We will discuss the pros and cons of a workplace romance in greater detail in chapter 6. Should touch be considered accidental until proven otherwise? Only you can be the judge of the intent of a touch.

Penny once worked for a company that expected frontal hugging on greeting and exiting. For some individuals this was uncomfortable. She noticed that those who were uncomfortable with hugging did not continue employment with this company for prolonged periods of time before moving on. The work setting has become an area of concern when it comes to touch because of all the laws now in place for sexual discrimination and harassment. You should always take great care that touch in the workplace is clearly nonsexual to avoid employment issues. Some people just need to take a deep breath and realize that not all touch in the workplace has sexual connotations.

Relationships at work are complicated and carry deep implications and risks. One or both of you could possibly lose your job with a workplace romance. It becomes difficult to work with someone and trust them at work if you have suffered a broken heart in a relationship. Trust, safety, and feelings become central issues that reduce office efficiency. The broken relationship damage can extend to office friendships that become polarized and make the work environment a living nightmare for you and others with all the drama that unfolds as coworkers take sides and alliances form. Exercise extreme care in workplace romances, or, better yet, avoid them altogether.

Touch has a very special place in a relationship. When deep love is shared between two persons, touch is a mighty expression of that love in an intimate way. It allows couples to give and receive pleasure while communicating. When relationships have progressed to sexual expression, all forms of touch can be used to provide excitement toward a progression to sexual intercourse. This path to intimacy includes all forms of touch, including facial nuzzles, kissing, and caressing each other. The final phase, lovemaking, is the culmination of all touches and includes tactile stimulation during foreplay known as the light or protopathic touch. With your soul mate, there is complete openness, lack of fear, and communicating through intimate touch. Bonding emotionally, physically, and spiritually is strengthened in a committed relationship with touch. Touch of this magnitude will allow a giving and receiving of pleasure. Touch communication at this level is special and beyond words. It requires commitment, trust, safety, and openness. This touch can be heated and passionate or teasing and playful. Touching of this nature is a time to draw close in a way that cannot be done with anyone other than your soul mate. This is why sexual intimacy or intercourse is a very special gift when shared with someone you care about. With your soul mate there is a trust in touching each other and fulfilling your partner's physical desire and knowing that your physical needs are being met also. This is the circle or cycle of loving touch that is given without expectations. It always returns to you as a satisfying experience. Sexual intercourse does not constitute love or this level of caring. For some it is a selfish act to fulfill personal desires and there is not a connection or fulfillment as a soul mate.

Touch is not always pleasurable for some people. Skin-to-skin contact can bring about anxiety, fear, and shame if there is a lack of confidence or a body image dislike. There are also some physical problems, such as neuropathy, that cause pain with touch. Common life occurrences impact our ability to feel comfortable in our own skin. The aging process impacts our bodies, and we gain weight, the skin sags, and muscles are not as robust or become flabby. Childbirth changes a woman's body. Illness and stress can impact the physical body, causing changes such as weight gain, weight loss, change of hair texture, drier or oilier skin, acne, loss of body parts due to disease, or loss of bodily functions. To feel comfortable with touch, you will need to change the things you do not like, or accept the things you cannot change.

With your soul mate it is possible to express total acceptance and support. Any feelings of fear or apprehension may be calmed through touching such as kissing, nuzzling, and a gentle massage. This is deeply intimate and is designed to draw the relationship closer together. If anxiety is felt during touch, you will need to explore your emotions associated with that touch. Hurt, fear, anger, bitterness, and distrust are some of the emotions that destroy a loving touch.

In today's society, movement of touch into the arousal and sexual stage happens much too quickly for most couples.

Physical intimacy and touch do not ensure or guarantee commitment or emotional bonding.

Communication through touch can be giving or very self-serving, depending on the individual. This is often a source of miscommunication between couples and results in hurt emotions and spirits. It is advised that you follow the biblical wisdom of establishing an emotional, spiritual, and intellectual commitment that includes marriage before stimulating touch is explored as a couple. This is a foundational principle for dating backward. For personal integrity, you may want to consider limiting touch to holding hands, hugging, and simple kissing. We should all know where our limits of temptation are and be very careful not to get too close to those boundaries. In addition, it can be beneficial to limit the amount of time you spend alone with a potential mate so that the temptation of physical intimacy is minimized. Spending time with other couples or in public places will limit your ability to be tempted. Once you have crossed that line, you can never undo it.

Unwritten rules of communication

We all have unwritten rules that we live by. One of the problems with communication is that so many people expect everyone to understand their unwritten rules of relationships even though these rules have not been communicated. We naturally assume that everyone's unwritten rules are the same as our own. What are unwritten rules? They are rules that we live our lives by daily. You may not even be aware of your unwritten rules. They are rules that you may have never made a conscious decision to adopt, but they exist. They can be deal breakers in relationships, and when these rules are violated it can signal the end of a relationship. One example of an unwritten rule might be that if you love me, you will never raise your voice to me. Communication could break down if one person was raised in a family that discussed issues calmly and quietly and their mate was raised in a loud, boisterous family and may have had to raise his or her voice just to be heard or to get their point across. This is one example of an unwritten rule that can generate a feeling that results in a deal breaker or the beginning of the end of the relationship.

Another unwritten rule might be that if you don't return my phone calls or e-mails on a timely basis, you are totally disrespecting me and I'm not that important to you. Potential conflict can arise here if the person calling or e-mailing has unrealistic expectations. What is considered a reasonable time frame? That acceptable time frame is variable from one person to another. There can be many reasons for a delayed response, including, but not limited to, unexpected work, family or other obligations, or distractions that may have come up. For some individuals it is a deal breaker, and there are no excuses that are acceptable with a delay in response. We all have these unwritten rules. The important thing is that you discover your unwritten rules, define them, understand them, and then communicate them to your mate. Unwritten rules can lead to the premature end of a relationship or be an adventure of sharing and discovery into the true nature of each other.

If you are truly honest with yourself as you go through the process of discovering your unwritten rules, you will probably discover that you have some rules about dating. If your rules are too restrictive or in conflict with each other, it may be that you may have significant problems maintaining any relationship for a long period of time. For example, if you want someone to shower you with attention, yet you want significant time to yourself or to be with friends, you could be sending mixed signals to the person you are dating. They may not understand when and where to shower you with attention. If they are not told about these rules, you both will get frustrated because you are not communicating your rules to each other.

If you have had multiple unsuccessful relationships and cannot figure out why, your rules may be the first place to look. If your rules are too restrictive or in conflict with each other, you may need to reevaluate your rules to see if they are truly realistic or an impediment to get what you ultimately are looking for: an extraordinary relationship.

Chapter 6

Conversations to have before
you get too serious

In the past two chapters we have discussed different types of communication. Now, let's discuss *what* to talk about. In an extraordinary relationship, or in your search for this relationship, all subjects should be on the table for discussion. They don't all need to be discussed on the first date, but they should be covered early on in your relationship.

The following subjects are some very important topics that need to be addressed. Some of these topics are very sensitive subjects and should be discussed tactfully and discreetly. Both parties should understand that the discussion is for your own information only. The information you learn about each other should not be shared with others unless you have specific permission to discuss it with someone else. Revealing confidential information to others or using the information to be hurtful during future conversations is certain to destroy any trust between you and will permanently damage or destroy your relationship. We cannot stress this point strongly enough.

Money

Money is one of the most important topics, one of the least discussed early in a relationship, and the cause of more breakups and divorce than any other subject. One of the first things you need to discover is whether your potential mate is financially stable. If they are working, are they saving money on a regular basis (at least monthly)? Do they use credit wisely, or do they have several credit cards all maxed out? Do they live paycheck to paycheck, or do they have money left over at their next payday? As the country song says, do they have "too much month at the end of the money"? Much of this information is available just by observation and watching how someone uses and spends money.

What is the person's attitude toward money? Is it a tool to get ahead? Is it something they idolized and can't get enough of? Is money basically meaningless and only for the "here and now"—if they have it, they spend it? These are important questions to understand. If you are frugal and spend wisely and your potential mate is a spendthrift, or vice versa, you are going to have problems, because one uses money wisely, the other has no respect for it, or the goals for money may be as different as night and day. This is a recipe for relationship disaster. Both of you should have a similar respect and goals for money. Healthy financial attitudes are living within your means, saving for your future, minimizing debt, giving generously, and having some enjoyment with money along the way.

Do you have to know the balance of someone's checking account? Not necessarily early in the relationship. But eventually it will be something you should know if you are in a serious, committed relationship. If you are with someone who is evasive or secretive about anything in his or her life, especially money, this should be a red flag for your relationship.

As you progress into a serious, long-term relationship, it is important to discuss management of finances. You will want to set goals and determine if boundaries exist, such as whether one of you will have more "control" of the money or if you will both have an equal say in how it is spent. If you progress into marriage, your assets should be combined. You both need to be working in the same direction financially. As a former financial adviser, Rick saw too many situations where spouses had separate personal checking accounts and separate assets. This did not promote trust or their ability to work together financially. In certain circumstances, such as a blended family situation, a prenuptial agreement may be appropriate. A detailed estate plan is also highly recommended. In both of these instances it is advisable to seek legal help.

Employment

In a relationship you will want to understand how and where financial stability is derived. This includes what a potential mate's attitude toward work is. This brings up the questions: Does the person you are interested in have a job? Are they gainfully employed or do they just drift from job to job? If he or she is unemployed, how long have they been unemployed? Are they seriously looking for work or are they "waiting for the right opportunity"? Are they self-employed? You will find that the work commitment for a successful self-employed individual will require a greater expenditure of time than a person who works 9-5pm. Or, is the person retired and living on retirement savings? A lot can be determined about someone's character by getting answers to these questions.

These are very important questions to ask and understand. As we mentioned earlier in this book, people who drift from job to job or are chronically unemployed may have emotional issues that need to be dealt with. If a person is employed but constantly complaining about their job, it may be that they have a terrible job or a terrible employer. However, the option exists for them to leave and find another job. In this situation, it may be a matter of that person just not having the ambition to seek better employment or just enjoy complaining about work. This type of negativity can very quickly suck the joy out of most relationships.

There is a small but growing percentage of people who have an income based on disability, and often it is hidden or covered as early retirement. This type of income is fixed, and there may be a disability associated with that person that creates a greater medical need and cost. Marriage may bring a financial burden to you or interrupt the other person's household income. This will need to be discussed openly and completely to allow you to understand the impact of a marriage relationship and health care commitments that you may be required to make.

There can also be issues with income involving disability. If your potential mate has a legitimate disability, they may be collecting income from insurance or government benefits or maybe both. As a former financial adviser, Rick has seen both legitimate and illegitimate claims. If the claims are legitimate, fine. However, character issues can be discovered if the person is working for cash or directing earned income through another person in order to be able to still collect disability benefits. If they are gaming the system, this is probably not the person you want to be with. People who are willing to commit fraud do not have strong morals and should not even be considered good dating prospects.

Self-employed people can present a different set of challenges. Many times, if they run a small business, entrepreneurs can spend significantly more than forty hours a week at their business. Fifty to sixty-hour weeks are not unheard of. The flip side of that coin is that if the business has become large enough and successful enough, the owner may have significant free time to pursue new activities and relationships. You have to understand and be accepting of the large time commitments the business owner has to his or her business.

If the person you are interested in is retired, there may be a couple of challenges there too. Yes, they will probably have a significant amount of free time, but that time may be committed to interests such as church, charities, family (children, grandchildren, etc.), or hobbies. Do you have similar interests? Are you still working? If you are, how will your time commitments be compatible with your mate's?

Finally, what do you bring to the table? Are you gainfully employed? Are you unemployed and waiting for the "right job" or a "management position" to come along? All of the questions asked above will apply to you as well. You must be willing to look at yourself objectively to determine if you are in a desirable position for a positive, financially healthy relationship. During your working years, employment can bring financial peace and stability to a relationship. The amount of money you earn is not as important as how you handle what you have.

Sex

Sex is always an important subject to discuss, but in the American culture it is rarely discussed openly within a relationship. Boundaries should be discussed, expressed, and respected. Pushing or violation of boundaries is a red flag and indicates an individual that will not continue to respect you later in the relationship. More times than not, sex is joked about or discussed very superficially, and rarely seriously and in depth. Trust and openness will allow you to discuss the fulfillment of fantasies and desires and to explore each other intimately and deeply through conversation. This is a subject that needs to be discussed seriously but with a bit of caution. Conversations outside of marriage about sexual desires and preferences can very easily become suggestive and ultimately physical if you are not careful.

Men and women differ when it comes to sexual intimacy. Most men are able to have sex without loving the person or feeling committed. Women most often connect sexual intimacy with love and commitment. These statements are thought to be the general rule but it is not always the case. When the relationship approaches or grows to intimate levels, there should be open discussion on the frequency of desire, what you will or will not allow, and your likes and dislikes. To avoid arguments later on, consider the following subject matter.

- How often sex should happen in a marriage.

- Whether both partners enjoy oral sex.

- Whether intercourse should occur during a menstrual cycle.

- Whether there is the expectation of an open relationship for partners other than each other.

- Whether any other personal issues on this topic need to be explored with each other.

The use of toys, bondage, spanking, and fetishes are but a few of the other issues to explore. Do you wait until marriage for intercourse, or do you have sex outside of marriage? You can never assume you understand what your partner does or does not like without discussion. You need to ask questions and verify your understanding.

How do you and your partner view sex in terms of frequency, need, and reason for intimate sharing? Is it approached as a release of stress, or is it approached as building excitement in a relationship? Problems can develop in relationships quickly if you enjoy the excitement and building of sexual tension and your partner looks at sexual relations for stress relief only. The two are polar opposites and will have a hard time coexisting. It will take time to build a sound relationship to discuss these issues and share openly and honestly with each other. It may take some counseling to discover what real feelings are associated with sexual intercourse.

Health

The topic of health has several different subcomponents to it. They include physical health, mental health, and spiritual health. These topics can be further subdivided into your current state of wellness and what you do to maintain or improve your health.

Health in general is an important topic to discuss, especially as you get older. In our early years of life, we typically have no health problems. With age, health issues start to creep into our lives. It could be any number of things, from high blood pressure, muscular aches and pains, and arthritis to more serious health issues such as heart disease, multiple sclerosis, cancer, erectile dysfunction, back problems, or female issues, to name just a few. There may even be sexually transmitted diseases with lifelong consequences that come into play. You should explore all medical issues completely. Medical health should be discussed early on in a relationship. As we have said, there should be no secrets, especially if you are contemplating a long-term relationship. You need to understand all relevant health issues that either one of you may have, because even though it may not be a significant issue in the present, it could have a significant impact on your relationship in the future.

Questions that come to mind are:

- Are you willing to be a primary caregiver in the event that certain diseases arise?

- Are you willing to not have sexual relations with a mate who has active STDs?

- What does the disease or illness mean and how will it impact you as an individual?

- Will you need to sacrifice personal time, efforts, needs, or desires because of the illness?

- How are the person's daily needs being met? What are those needs?

- Will the illness prevent the person from fulfilling needs that you have?

For example, can you do without sexual relations if your mate's back goes out for weeks at a time? They may not need significant care now, but in years to come could require constant, around-the-clock attention.

Sexually transmitted diseases (STDs) are a huge issue today with life-altering impact. Are you willing to limit some or all sexual activity if there are STDs present? Is your potential mate now disease free or is the disease dormant? Can you contract the disease by being with them? Will you need to use condoms forever? There are some STDs that require you to abstain from intercourse for prolonged periods of time, or you will need to use condoms as a protective measure to reduce the risk of transmission to you. Not all STDs are permanent and forever, but some are. You need to be prepared to discuss how this is going to impact your relationship because this will be different than that of the general population. Educate yourself on the STD and how it will impact your sexual relationship, including childbirth.

Physical and outdoor activities are important to some individuals. Is one or both of you physically active? Do you enjoy sharing common exercise routines, or are you a loner in exercise? Do you like the same type of exercise and want a mate that can join you in the gym, jogging, bicycling, kayaking, skiing, or other similar activities? Do you like camping, hunting, or other outdoor activities, and are you interested in sharing these events together? What are your eating habits? Is healthy eating important to either one of you, or do you like to eat whatever you like whenever you want?

There are differing views on how health is maintained. Some individuals do not believe in seeing physicians and prefer to be treated with herbs and naturopathic medicine. When they get sick, how do they expect to be treated? Some people want to be left alone and others want to be coddled and treated like a child. Are you able to meet or tolerate those expectations? Frustration can be reduced and avoided if common ideals and practices in health are shared.

Religion

Religion is one of the two topics that it is said should never be discussed if you want to maintain a friendship or relationship.

We respectfully disagree. If you are going to be in a long-term relationship with someone, this topic will most certainly come up at some point. Having open and honest conversations about your religious or spiritual beliefs is very important. One of the last things you want to do is to get deeply involved with someone only to find out that they have completely different views about religion than you. We believe it is important to be "equally yoked". If you are not believing similarly and working in the same direction spiritually, you start to create a chasm in your relationship. For example, if believing in Christ and going to church on a regular basis is important to you, having a mate that is a non-believer will create tension in your relationship that can ultimately tear it apart.

Common beliefs are that your mate will change if they watch you or that you can change them to believe as you do. The question becomes, do you want to spend a significant amount of time trying to convince someone that they need to change, or do you want to be with someone who naturally believes as you do? Is it impossible for a relationship to survive if two people have different beliefs? No. However, it becomes much more difficult because it increases the number of points of contention and introduces friction into the relationship. If you believe it is your mission to convert people to your belief, then become a missionary. Don't try to convert the person you think might be a potential mate.

Religious differences become difficult with holidays, special occasions such as baptisms, or special religious ordinances. Finding a partner who will share a similar or the same belief system as you will prevent this conflict. It is interesting to hear stories of how those who believed they were soul mates walked away from a relationship because of a conflict in spiritual beliefs. The pain of walking away was replaced with a joy untold when they found their soul mates and connected in all aspects, including a spiritual connection.

Politics

Politics is the second topic that is commonly suggested should never be discussed if you want to maintain a friendship or relationship. Again, we respectfully disagree. Religion and politics are two very important issues that guide an individual and frame the home and society. We believe you should hold similar beliefs if you want to have a successful and extraordinary relationship. Conservatives should be with conservatives, moderates with moderates, and liberals with liberals. By being on the same page politically, you drastically reduce the number of potential arguments that can arise. Is it possible to be in a relationship with someone who does not believe as you do? Sure, but both people involved must love a good discussion and debate and agree to disagree forever. This is very difficult, if not impossible, to sustain long term. If politics are not important to you, then it can probably work if you do not have compatible views. You can agree to disagree. However, if this is a subject that you believe strongly in, then there will be friction whenever this topic comes up. Can you avoid this topic altogether? Of course you can. The problem then is that you cannot have extraordinary communication because this topic becomes an off-limits subject.

Household responsibilities

The topic of household responsibilities may seem a little odd at first, but the reality is that if you intend to be in a long-term relationship, especially if it is leading to marriage, this is an important subject. The subjects of who cooks, who cleans, who does laundry, who irons are important to address. How many times have we heard women say, "He won't lift a finger around the house to help me. He expects me to work all day, come home and cook, and help the kids with their homework, and then wonders why I'm too tired to make love to him!" Before you get yourself in this situation, it is important to have a conversation about household responsibilities. Who will do what around the house? Do you share responsibilities? Do you each take on responsibility for certain chores each week? Do you hire someone to come in and help with some of the household chores so that you have more time for each other and your family? Does one of you work outside the home and earn the household income and the other stay home and take care of the household duties? There are countless ways of answering these questions. The key is to have the discussion and figure out the arrangements that work best for your situation.

What about personal household habits? Do you leave clothes lying on the floor, or are they in a hamper? Do you squeeze the toothpaste tube from the bottom or from the middle of the tube? Do you put the toilet paper roll on to unroll from the front or from the back? Do you toss bags in the corner that are filled with purchases from the store because you are too lazy to put them away? Do these sound like silly or ridiculous questions? Yes, they do. To many people the answers are unimportant. Yet to others, the answers are very important. In the short term they will have very little impact on your life. However, twenty years from now, the answers may make the difference between an extraordinary relationship and doing hard time for murder! While we are exaggerating (only slightly) here, the aggravation of being married to someone who has polar opposite habits can be frustrating, unpleasant, and unproductive in a relationship.

As you are getting to know each other, you will be able to tell a lot about how much each of you is willing to do just by observing how the other lives. If both of you are neat and your homes are well maintained, you might expect that you will have a mate who is willing to help around the house or that they may desire to hire someone to help. On the other hand, if one of you is messy and the other is neat, the neat person should not expect any significant help, because household chores are not a priority to the messy person. Are these observations absolute? Not at all. However, they are a pretty good indicator of what you could expect if you were to marry and move in together.

To improve communication in this area, you need to understand that individuals should function in the roles of giver and taker. Both persons should be fair in sharing the household duties and function in both roles. To not do so can create a disproportional burden on one partner or the other. In an extraordinary relationship, there is a natural flow to the giving and taking. It is balanced. If the situation becomes unbalanced, both partners need to feel comfortable about expressing their concern or frustration.

Terminating communication

There comes a time in less-than-extraordinary relationships when you need to decide the relationship is over. We are blinded to certain realities of toxic relationships because we get so wrapped up in the problems of everyday life. We have to step back and look at what these toxic relationships are doing to us. It may seem very mature to want to "remain friends." Hanging on and staying in contact, even after you have broken up or divorced, prevents you from moving on to a healthy relationship. This would be like noticing that your house is on fire and staying inside the house trying to put out the fire even though the fire is out of control. You are much better off leaving the burning house (relationship) and letting it burn to the ground than trying to remain inside and perish (emotionally).

In Rick's coaching experience, he has found that one of the biggest mistakes we make (men and women) is to stay in contact with an ex-boyfriend, ex-girlfriend, or ex-spouse, especially if it was a toxic relationship. By remaining in regular contact, you maintain ties that prevent you from being able to fully and freely move on into a new and healthy relationship. The one exception about breaking off total communication is if you have children with your ex. If your ex is actively involved with your children, there will need to be some maintenance of communication. It should be limited to issues involving the children and nothing more. As the children grow into adulthood, the communication with your ex can be minimized and limited to only topics relating to the children. One woman told Rick that after only forty-eight hours of not replying to unnecessary and unwanted communication from her ex, she felt as if she had been freed. She hadn't realized how emotionally binding and restrictive communications with her ex-spouse were. Rick has had similar responses from women who had continued to reply to unwanted communications from ex-boyfriends. You have to understand that just the fact that you respond, even if it is insulting or sarcastic, opens the door to further communication, and pretty soon you have let yourself get sucked back into a relationship that is like a black hole in space. It sucks the light and life out of everything in its vicinity.

It may be a little easier to sever the communication connection with someone from a toxic relationship than with someone from an "OK" relationship. It is much harder to break communication with someone who is a decent person but not your soul mate. Many times we can get drawn back into communications because the ex is not a bad person. He or she may have flaws that are deal breakers that we just cannot live with. It is easy to fall back into contact with these people, especially when we are feeling a little lonely or would like a conversation with someone familiar. Regardless of what your former relationship was like, you need to focus on what is in your best interest. Breaking ties to relationships that are less than extraordinary is necessary to be available for the right person to come into your life.

This way you can enjoy an extraordinary relationship when you find the right person. You are not available to find the right person if you remain attached in any way to any previous relationship.

One of the most amusing comments I have heard is to set a time limit on avoiding communication with someone from a toxic relationship. That would be like an alcoholic saying they are going to remain sober for six months and then take a drink. Well, it isn't long before they are drunk again and the cycle starts all over. The same is true for past relationships; once the ties are broken, they need to remain broken. Once communication has ended, don't reopen it. Move on and don't look back. Your future is ahead of you...not behind you.

If you get nothing else out of this book, please learn to communicate well. Time and again we have seen amazing growth in one or both partners in a relationship when communication is open and honest. This is simply the most crucial component of any extraordinary relationship. All of the other aspects of a relationship are building blocks that must be laid on the foundation of extraordinary communication.

Chapter 7

The Four Cornerstones of Relationships

How do you know when your relationship is right or an extraordinary soul mate kind of relationship? There are Four Cornerstones that can help you figure that out. The four cornerstones that we have identified are spiritual, emotional, intellectual, and physical. Are these four points of connection a guarantee to an extraordinary relationship? Absolutely not, but it is a good start in the right direction. There are many other factors involved, including extraordinary communication and speaking your mate's primary love languages, as mentioned in earlier chapters. The Four Relationship Cornerstones are more like the foundation of a home. They are the building blocks on which you want to build the rest of your relationship. Let's take a look at each of these key areas one at a time. They are not listed in any particular order, and one does not necessarily rate higher in importance than any other. If you are missing any one or more of these cornerstones, it will not be an extraordinary relationship.

Spiritual Cornerstone

We believe the spiritual cornerstone is of critical importance. A relationship struggles if the two people are not on the same page spiritually. What does that mean? It means that you need to have the same fundamental belief in religion, God, and the afterlife. For example, soul mates will have the same or similar beliefs, whether it is Christianity, Judaism, or whatever else you may believe spiritually. You don't necessarily need to be in the same place in your spiritual journey at the same time, but you should have similar beliefs and be moving in the same direction. The Bible speaks of being equally yoked. This means having similar views and working to grow knowledge and wisdom in the same direction. Growth and change that moves a couple in different directions spiritually only separates them and does not hold the relationship together. If you don't believe in God or are agnostic, you need to search out someone who is of similar belief. We believe that not being on the same page spiritually is a critical mistake. Your spiritual connection is foundational to a strong, loving relationship.

Some of the greatest divisiveness in a relationship comes from a lack of common spiritual ground. We have all heard of the couples who fell in love and one is of one faith and the other has a vastly different belief structure. The relationship is OK for a while, until one mate has to start compromising their beliefs in order to keep peace in the relationship. Often what transpires is that a division or wall is created between you as a couple. The person of faith attends church (or synagogue or another holy place) alone, with each going his or her own individual way.

Different belief systems will become an even greater struggle when there are children involved. Will the children be raised in one religion or the other or both? How do you decide? Who has to compromise? Who has to give up their beliefs? What message is being sent to the children if only one parent has and practices religious beliefs? Intentionally or not, one person undermines the beliefs of the other. I (Penny) have witnessed families and relationships struggling with differences in values. These differences were not so big at first, but grew over time to destroy the marriage and relationship. Some of these differences were a lack of support for special occasions such as baptism, confirmation, holiday celebrations, or spiritual achievements. Extraordinary relationships exist when there is a shared excitement, success, and growth. Relationships do not fully develop when spiritual values differ, and the result is a stagnation of the relationship. Often there are hurts, bitterness, resentment, anger, or neglected feelings that can result as an outcome of these differences.

There are times when two people care for each other and they are on a spiritual discovery and seeking change in their current belief system. Divergent beliefs are not *always* a bad thing if you are helping a nonbeliever to become a true believer. Extreme caution is advised in a relationship at this point. This can foster an unhealthy relationship with feelings of inferiority or superiority between each other. This results in a foundational loss and begins to decay the relationship. If the believer is not extremely firm in their beliefs, the change could go the other way and the believer could become a nonbeliever. Either way, this situation brings a lot of friction to a relationship, and it is better not to enter a relationship with such divergent beliefs. It is a challenging and a difficult journey that can be filled with disappointments.

When you are dating, conversations need to be had regarding spiritual beliefs. These conversations need to be in-depth conversations. In addition, you need to observe your potential mate's actions.

Are their actions consistent with what they say? I (Penny) have experienced awkward moments when I have stopped to offer grace over a meal and the other person did not share the same level of commitment to pray in public. Fundamental differences can trigger feelings of embarrassment, anger, or any number of emotions.

Some (but not all) of the questions you might think about include:

- Can you have a great, deep, uplifting, and supportive conversation about your beliefs?

- Do you study your religion together?

- Do you fundamentally disagree and have little or no common spiritual ground?

- Do you share common beliefs?

- What are the differences in your beliefs?

- Do you pray together?

- How do you feel when they speak their mind in public or to another person?

Negative emotions or feelings associated with these questions can be a wakeup call to the existence of values that are vastly different and can result in the destruction of the relationship over time.

In addition to shared spiritual values and beliefs, what is necessary to have a strong spiritual connection? Prayer, study, fasting, and worship together are basic for a spiritual connection. Spiritual maturity and hearing God's voice together is a wonderful place to find your relationship. I (Penny) have experienced a spiritual connection so strong with a soul mate that we understood each other emotionally and spiritually. There were times when we both understood the direction God was taking our life together...*wow!* I can tell you that miracles happen as couples hear and follow the leadings of the Holy Spirit together and there is closeness with their soul mate that is like no other.

As an individual you have certain spiritual beliefs, and your mate will have their own spiritual beliefs. If their beliefs are not in alignment, relationship friction will occur. The spiritual connection you have as a couple can directly impact your social groups and friends. A difference in beliefs as a couple can bring challenges to you as an individual. As a couple you will generally share friends who most likely will hold your core values.

Search for that spiritual connection that helps generate and maintain an extraordinary relationship. Yes, an extraordinary relationship will require work and maintenance, but not as much as one that is less than extraordinary.

Intellectual Cornerstone

The intellectual cornerstone is not necessarily about education. It can be, but not necessarily. It is more about thinking along the same lines politically, financially, and socially. Does this mean you need to like exactly the same things, do the same things, or have the same level of education? No. What it does mean is that you can have great conversations about very difficult subjects or just talk about the weather or other everyday things and be on the same page. It also allows you to have great communication, as mentioned earlier. There is a respect for each other's intellect, for each other's experience, for each other's opinions. You are supportive of the other's hobbies or interests. One of the greatest examples I (Rick) can think of is when I met my first soul mate (yes, I believe we can have more than one). She told me of some of the things she was passionate about. I chuckled and said that she was on her own and that I would never be involved with such a frivolous activity. Yet, a couple of months later, I found myself actually becoming involved in a peripheral supportive way. As I learned more about this "frivolous" activity I came to appreciate all that was involved, things that most people would never know or understand unless they became involved in the activity. To this day, I still maintain a passing interest because of what she taught me. We believe that with your soul mate, this connection is so strong that you learn to understand your mate intimately, and this knowledge comes very quickly—in a matter of weeks or just a few short months. Does this mean that you will understand every facet of their life and come to know everything that he or she knows? Absolutely not! You will, however, have a greater understanding of this person than virtually anyone else, including family and lifelong friends.

Intellectual knowledge is not necessarily acquired. What we are suggesting is that it can be almost intuitive, as if you have known each other for a lifetime. You get each other's jokes and humor. You understand and share similar backgrounds or interests. From time to time, the older you get, you will cross paths with people like this. You may connect with a person in an instant, maybe only on an intellectual level. You will get the feeling that they could have been in your life for years but have only recently arrived. These connections are unique, rare and should be cherished.

When you have this connection with your soul mate, it elevates your relationship to another level. You are both individuals, and together you become extraordinary with the connections and love you share. The intellectual cornerstone allows you to look at your mate and instinctively understand where they are coming from, and there does not have to be much explanation. You know what they are thinking or where he or she is going with their thoughts. Some soul mates can even complete a sentence or thoughts for each other. You are not carbon copies of each other, but unique individuals who are different and connected in an extraordinary way.

Emotional Cornerstone

The emotional cornerstone creates an amazing connection. It is the one connection that is most often misunderstood, and, like the other cornerstones, it cannot stand alone to make an extraordinary relationship. This cornerstone is subject to your physical and mental health and hormones. This connection is the energy and binding strength of a relationship that is intertwined through the other three cornerstones. You can choose to be emotionally connected or not. That is why you may have heard that love is a choice.

Physical connection is tied with your emotional connection. Hormones are released as you look on how beautiful your mate is, and they trigger a response in which your heart beats quickly and excitement enters. You feel this as infatuation at the beginning of a relationship. It is the feeling you both get when you spot the other walking into the room. It is what makes your heart skip a beat or beat faster with excitement and anticipation of the next time you get to see each other. This emotional connection will cause your hands to sweat and knees to shake when you look at or think about this person. It is also that feeling you have after infatuation has passed that you can't wait to get home to share your day with your mate. It is the excitement you get when you hold hands, are in a long embrace, or snuggle up on the couch watching a movie. It is an energy that can be felt and not seen. You know and can feel your soul mate's energy in a room without touching each other.

How does the emotional cornerstone provide the glue for spiritual and intellectual connections? You share feelings of excitement, joy, and happiness with each other and for each other. This emotional connection is what brings you joy for your mate and their growth and accomplishments. You are happy when they are happy. You feel sorrow when they feel sorrow. You feel their success and pride in their accomplishments. You know and feel his or her emotions and feelings as if they were your own. You share and feel the love they have for God and others, and it is as if you are one. Both Penny and Rick have experienced an emotional connection of this type. It is beyond infatuation and extraordinary in how it brings a fullness and expansion to your life.

I (Penny) was having a conversation with a friend who was sorrowful that the infatuation stage was leaving her relationship after six months. Her fear was that the excitement would disappear and she would become bored. Infatuation and excitement are always present when something is new. Things such as a new car, boat, or household bring great excitement, but soon the newness wears off as you become familiar. Emotional relationships grow and change with the aging of the relationship. Your emotional ties to your mate become more precious to you. The thought of life without him or her is distressing. Losing your soul mate would be like the loss of an arm or leg. You care for them so deeply that to hurt them would be the same as hurting yourself. You are both individuals but united as one. Together you are better than alone as individuals. Relationship math is $1 + 1 = 1^{10}$ in an extraordinary relationship. I know a couple who are soul mates, and after sixty-five years of marriage he said, "I want to live three days longer than her." That struck me as an odd request that was very exact, and I asked him, "Why?" He said, "To make sure she gets buried correctly, and I have no reason to live after that." How beautiful is that deep, abiding, emotional bond between soul mates. Infatuation and excitement is just the beginning of the adventure of a lifetime. When you find your soul mate, infatuation will be transformed. You will find a deep, abiding, emotional bond to carry you through life's adventures together.

Many times you share similar feelings at the same time. At other times you are in different emotional places. The emotional cornerstone allows you to share emotional strength and support. Oftentimes one mate will be emotionally strong when the other is weak. At other times, the partners will exchange roles. You both will share strengths and weaknesses at different times. You will share love, joy, happiness, sadness, grief, pain, frustration, pride, excitement, to name just a few. It is almost instinctive for soul mates to be able to read each other's moods or emotions. It may be through facial expressions, body language, or verbal cues that your mate gives. Sometimes you just need to ask what they need from you, but more likely you ask for validation of what you already know and feel.

We don't want to create the impression that there won't be any emotional roller-coaster rides. In a true soul mate relationship, there will always be obstacles that get in your way. Life happens! There's nothing any of us can do to change that. And with a strong, loving, emotional bond, the two of you will weather life's upsets much more gracefully together than apart.

The foundation of the emotional cornerstone is emotional maturity. You need to understand who you are and what you need in a mate. As we discussed in chapter 3, if you are emotionally immature, or emotionally unavailable, you will be searching for the wrong elements in a relationship. When you are emotionally healthy and emotionally mature, you will be able to give fully of yourself and not hold anything back. This point is critical to a healthy relationship. If you hold back emotionally, you will be holding back the entire relationship. You have to be willing to be vulnerable, knowing full well that there is a possibility of being hurt.

Physical Cornerstone

Finally, there is the physical cornerstone. There are two components to a physical connection. Most of us immediately think of physical intimacy: touching, fondling, and making love. While that is a major part of an extraordinary relationship, there is more. In a healthy relationship, the first part of the connection is physical attraction. This is a key component to any physical connection. This is the part that can encompass the visual aspect of beauty. If there is physical attraction, it is usually almost instantaneous. If you are not attracted to a person, there is little likelihood that any serious relationship will develop. Rick had a conversation with a young woman during the writing of this book. She was an unwed mother of two and struggling with a relationship with the father of her children. She said he was a good man, a great father, and she really loved him as a person. He loved her as well and was doing everything he could to be with her. However, she was not physically attracted to him. Had there not been children involved, the decision would have been easy. For the children's sake, she should have stayed with him. Sadly, at the time this was written, she chose a different path.

Penny knows of several individuals who have stated that initially they were not physically attracted with fireworks in their soul for their mate, but they found that attraction to grow over time to an increased intensity of fireworks. The common factor is that their soul mates came in a physical package they did not expect. They were taller, shorter, more muscular, less muscular, than what they thought was their dream package. For them these minor differences in physical appearance were not deal breakers, given that they found everything else they were looking for. However, in most cases, the initial physical impression is the one that remains.

The physical cornerstone also includes nonsexual touch, such as holding hands, hugging, and kissing. It is thought that touch stimulates the release of oxytocin and strengthens the emotional connection with your soul mate. Energy is shared; connections are established and maintained through non intimate touch.

While any relationship starts to grow, the physical connection also starts to grow. If physical intimacy is introduced too soon, it will retard the growth and depth of the intellectual, spiritual, and emotional cornerstones. For men, sex stunts the brain and all but stops the learning curve. The introduction of sex can also take away from the budding relationship because there is a hollow, empty feeling after the fact. Most men walk away and need space after sex when there is no emotional connection or committed relationship. Ideally, you won't introduce sex into your relationship until your wedding night.

The Four Cornerstones in an extraordinary relationship are like the four legs of a table. When you have all four legs solidly connected to the table, it is an extremely stable platform. The same is true for a relationship. With all four "legs" (intellectual, spiritual, emotional, and physical) firmly in place, you have the foundation for a strong relationship. However, if you remove just one leg from the table, you instantly lose some of the stability and your relational foundation is weakened. If you remove a second leg, at best you will have a precarious balancing act. Finally, if you remove a third leg, you will have no stability or ability to support the relationship. The one-legged table (relationship) is typically what you end up with if you start a relationship based on the physical (sex) only. An extraordinary relationship is experiencing the Four Relationship Cornerstones, where you will find a love and joy that will last, grow, and sustain you for all of your life.

Chapter 8

Dating and finding your soul mate

Congratulations on making it this far in the book. Needing, wanting, and sharing love are the reasons we seek to find our soul mates. In the earlier chapters we discussed the importance of knowing yourself and loving yourself in order to love others. This is critically important as you move forward with your life. We both believe that first and foremost you need to know and love God. It is from your loving relationship with God that you can love yourself and extend that love to others. Dating is the process in which you sort through your relationships with others in the effort to find and share that love with your soul mate. The excitement is about to begin as you actively look for your soul mate.

You will be using all of the information that you have learned to this point, including your Must Have and Deal Breakers lists, to help guide you in the right direction to ultimately find your soul mate. Dating is putting the first seven chapters of this book into the action of finding your soul mate. Your soul mate is a person with whom you have a special relationship that has great communication with spiritual, intellectual, emotional, and physical connections. Life is filled with all types of relationships. Not all relationships are created equal or have potential in being your soul mate. Penny has seen many people spend copious amounts of time on dating acquaintances, only to find that it was time wasted and time lost looking for their soul mate. This chapter describes a process to help you sort through your old, current, and future relationships with the hopes that you will not lose precious time on a relationship that is going nowhere and lacks extraordinary qualities.

There are three major types of relationships: acquaintances, friendships, and courtships (intimate friendships). These three relationships are vastly different and yet interconnected. This interconnection will be explained as we explore the differences and growth of relationships. A relationship can be as simple as an interaction with the person taking your coffee order or as complex as being connected within all Four of the Relationship Cornerstones. The ever-present danger is in getting stuck in an acquaintance or friendship relationship thinking it is leading to something more and having your time wasted. Sorting friendships into categories of acquaintances, friendships, and courtships seems cold and analytical, but it is helpful to look at these categories objectively when making life-altering decisions. Making the decision for relationship change requires boundaries, goals, and direction in your life. These are difficult decisions that can have deep consequences. We will also make you aware of some of the pitfalls to watch out for in friendships and introduce some techniques to help and guide you about where to look to help improve your probability of success. Ultimately we can only provide you with a process to guide you. You must put in the effort to make life changes to bring your ideal relationship into a reality.

Acquaintance, friendship, and courtship

All relationships begin with interaction between two people to get acquainted. All relationships start as acquaintances. This is a very beginning and basic level of relationship. You might know someone by name or by sight and acknowledge them as you pass on the street. Most conversations will be superficial in nature. They may be limited to "Hi. How are you?" or "Nice weather we're having, isn't it?" Sometimes these superficial conversations can grow into somewhat deeper conversations.

Electronic dating sites help break the ice by providing some information in a profile to help you determine if this is a person who possesses qualities on your Must Have list or who you can rule out due to a Deal Breaker. We want to caution you that anything written is just that, words on a page. You need to make the effort to invest time in getting to know the individual before you jump to the conclusion that you will be soul mates prior to meeting.

Asking great questions and being a good listener can help you determine if you want the relationship to grow into something more than an acquaintance. At this point your relationship could go in one of three directions. It could move you further apart, in which case the acquaintanceship will end; it could remain where it is; or, if there is interest from both parties, it could move to friendship.

If the relationship moves to the friendship stage, you will start to gain greater knowledge and understanding of each other. This is the point in a relationship when you start to learn how many connections you have with each other. You will discover basic or common shared interests and concerns. You have the freedom to explore opinions, ideas, wishes, and goals. You will discover if you love each other for who you really are and if there is potential for a life together ahead. Taking your self-assessment, Must Have, and Deal Breaker lists, you will begin to determine if this person has the qualities needed for an extraordinary relationship that is based on the Four Cornerstones of Relationships. If there are not enough must haves or there are any deal breakers present, it is time to end the relationship. It is your choice to choose to keep the relationship as an acquaintance, casual friendship, or close friendship. However, this can be a tricky situation if you choose to maintain anything more than a casual friendship. You want to be emotionally available for your soul mate. Maintaining close friendships can possibly hinder your future relationships because you may not be emotionally available. If you each have enough of the other's must haves, you have a relationship that has the potential of moving to the close and intimate friendship or courtship level.

When you find yourself at the point of moving your relationship to the intimate friend or courtship level, you become exclusive in your dating. *Courting* is an old term used for two individuals who have declared that they are no longer seeking the attention of other individuals. They are choosing to be devoted to each other in an attempt to support each other and begin a life together. This is why we encourage you to date many people in casual friendships. To limit your options and restrict friendships will close down possible avenues for finding your soul mate. During courtship, you spend more time together, getting to know each other's more intimate characteristics. You will learn how to comfort each other through trials and sorrows. There is a commitment of faithfulness, loyalty, and availability to them alone. Together you begin planning a future. There may be struggles and challenges that arise to keep emotional excitement alive as the infatuation wears off and life together is beginning to take shape.

Courtship or intimate friendship is the time you will begin to pour your energy into that one relationship. It is during this time that the circle of friends of both mates begins to meld together. You both will gain and lose friends during this time, and the only friendships that remain are nonsexual in nature and can be shared with your soul mate.

The time it takes to develop each of the different levels of relationships can vary in length from a few seconds to a few hours to several months or years. As you evaluate your friendships and relationships objectively, you will begin to place them in a category of acquaintance, friend, or courtship (intimate friend, of which you should have only one at a time). You can learn a lot about yourself as you do this. Some people choose to focus on having many acquaintances but have few close friends. Others choose to focus more on close friends and have fewer acquaintances. Individuals with large numbers of acquaintances and very busy social schedules are opposite in personality of those who have a few close friendships. Those personalities who like to spend most of their social time with a few close friends do not feel the need to seek out new acquaintances. How you socialize and spend your time can create friction and misunderstanding if you are not on the same page. By looking at how you like to spend your time socializing with acquaintances, casual friends, or close friends, you will have a better understanding of yourself and what to look for in a potential mate. If you look at what your percentage or ratio of acquaintances to close friends is, you will discover something about your personality. If you look at his or her mixture of friendships, you will understand more about your potential mate's personality also. There is no right or wrong ratio of acquaintances to close friends because each person is unique with unique needs. This is just a way to help you better understand yourself, your potential mate, and friendship structure and how it impacts your relationship.

Physical intimacy

Physical intimacy can present itself at any point in any relationship and should be reserved for the bonds of marriage. Unfortunately, in today's society it is becoming rarer and rarer to find couples who actually wait for marriage. This is especially true with people who have been married one or more times. There are a lot of reasons to rationalize this, but one of the most common reasons we hear is that people want to make sure they are with a mate that will satisfy them in bed. We caution you on this line of thinking and rationalization. For every decision and action, there are consequences associated as an outcome of your choices and actions. We are going to explore the reasons not to become physically intimate and the problems that can occur if you are.

When you find that special someone you desire to share physical intimacy with, it is a game changer and changes the focus of the relationship. One-night stands or new relationships that become sexually involved immediately or early on are usually short-lived. Emotions and connections become entangled and blurry. Communication suffers, and there is little more than physical attraction and nothing else to build on. Premature physical intimacy will prevent you from fully discovering and developing your intellectual, spiritual, and emotional connections. The relationship stalls, with the end coming quickly. We know people who have had a great friendship and introduced sexual intercourse into the relationship, which then destroyed the friendship. Physical intimacy is never a way to guarantee the progress toward love. We would like to encourage you to grow a nonsexual relationship first when dating. Early sexual intimacy in a relationship can seal the death of a relationship, and this type of dating will be emotionally painful as relationships move in and out of your life.

You can protect your heart, soul, and health by not entering into sexual relationships with strangers or casual or even close friends. Can you stand to lose a good friend for a night of pleasure? You are in control, in charge of and responsible for your actions, and will have to endure the outcomes of your behavior. Individual social values of what is acceptable are blurred in today's society. Having sexual relationships with multiple partners is acceptable in some social circles, and open relationships exist. Drama, anxiety, and stress are experienced with individuals who practice this lifestyle. This book is not intended to pass judgment on this kind of lifestyle, but to share with you what is experienced by those who are exhausted and desire an intimate one-on-one relationship. Multiple partners and early physical intimacy can result in many friendships that are short-lived, a sense of anxiety, fear of loss, loneliness, and a wanting that is unsatisfied. The physical body can respond in the following ways: insomnia, headaches, stomach and intestinal problems, tremors in hands or legs, weakness, increased infections due to a diminished immune system, weight gain or loss, poor concentration, poor memory, and even hair loss, just to name a few.

The world teaches you to have sex first to check out a potential mate. By doing so, this is where the relationship damage begins. Having sex before you are married or before you connect with your mate intellectually, emotionally, and spiritually is like having dessert before your meal. Physical intimacy should be like the icing on the cake, or the capstone to the relationship. By waiting, you will create stronger bonds and deeper communication within your relationship. By dating backward, you will develop many strong friendships and not destroy people and their emotions along the way by having sex too soon.

So how do you or can you exercise control and responsibility when faced with passion? It is simple. Think it thorough. The red flag you should recognize is when you feel the desire to become physically intimate with an individual. This is when you need to ask yourself the hard questions: Where will physical intimacy take this relationship? When the relationship changes, am I willing to risk the loss of the friendship? Am I moving toward a one-on-one relationship with this individual? What do I or we stand to gain by adding physical intimacy to the relationship at this time?

You need to consider these issues before you can seriously consider moving into an exclusive, monogamous relationship. If you cannot control your urges, then you have no business claiming to want to be in a monogamous relationship or seeking one. Adults and teens alike suffer the same consequences of multiple sexual partners. Being honest with yourself and where you are with your sexuality and control is foundational for extraordinary relationships. If you are on a dating site, then post the truth. If you are seeking a marriage or serious long-term relationship, do not push for sexual intimacy early on. And if you are dating someone like this, it is time to leave that relationship and move on to someone who is more stable and trustworthy. True love waits, and it is extraordinary when that level of respect and love is given and received.

When you are ready for a serious, long-term, monogamous relationship, be prepared for your circle of friends to change, and for the potential drama that goes with this change. As your relationship matures and life as a couple begins, your circle of friends will begin to change. Some changes will be good and some will be difficult to deal with. The positive friendships that you both maintain should be the ones you nurture and cherish. They will be the ones that give you the most support and will be the most honest with you if they see questionable things going on within your life.

The first date

There is a difference in first dates based on whether you are meeting someone for the first time or whether you are on a first date with a casual acquaintance. The experience of "the first date" will most likely happen many times over while seeking to find your soul mate. The first date is defined as where you meet alone for the first time face-to-face. This meeting can be fraught with varying levels of anxiety because there are different kinds of first dates. Some first dates you will have invested time in phone conversations, e-mail, texting, or group interactions, and you may already have connections with this individual. This will cause your anxiety to be of a different kind than a first date with someone you have never met. If this is your first time to meet someone who you know little or nothing about, in essence the first date is a first interview, just like a job interview. You are both interviewing the other to determine if you are compatible. Does this date have to be an interrogation? Absolutely not! However, it can be if that is your style, but it doesn't need to be. In fact it should be much more casual than an interview. Much of the time when I (Rick) am on a first date I try to let the conversation just flow. You can learn a lot about a person just by listening during a casual conversation. If the conversation lags at all, you can ask good, nonthreatening, probing, open-ended questions. Here are a few questions you might ask.

- What was your favorite vacation?

- What was your childhood like?

- How would your friends describe you to me?

- What are your favorite summertime/wintertime activities?

You get the idea. These are just a few questions to consider. You can come up with dozens more on your own. Each date will be different, so different questions may be needed for each one. If you find that the conversation lags at all or there is any significant "quiet time," this could be a signal that there may be a lack of connection in one or more of the Four Relationship Cornerstones: intellectual, emotional, spiritual, or maybe even physical.

One-sided love

Don't be misled by a one-sided love. This can occur when one person likes someone and wants to pursue the relationship more than the other person. He or she could attribute it to the belief they have found their soul mate when the other partner does not share the same feeling of connection. This is incredibly difficult for the person who feels the connection, and they could have a hard time letting go. The discomfort for the person who is not as invested comes from awkwardness and not wanting to hurt the other individual. This more often than not leads to hanging on to a relationship much longer than you should, or it can be seen as a stalking type of behavior. Communication is important to be able to say clearly that you are not interested or that you feel the relationship is one sided. You both need to be wise enough to recognize and acknowledge the desire of one and lack of desire by the other. One-sided love is more likely to occur if one person is not completely clear on what they are looking for or when one person is absolutely clear on what they are looking for in a mate and there is a disconnect with each other. This disconnect can also happen when someone is seeking a casual dating relationship and the other is seeking a long-term commitment.

It helps to clarify this intent with the interested person early on in the relationship. Are you both looking for a long-term, committed relationship, casual dating, or no commitment? This can be a serious disconnection for you both if you are not seeking the same kind of relationship. Do not assume his or her intent. You need to have a direct conversation on this matter, and it is best done in person to read their body language, facial expressions, and hear voice inflections. People can write words in a letter, e-mail, or text that portray one message, but when you see and hear it in person, another message is delivered.

If you are unclear about what you are looking for in a mate, it can be easy to fall for someone who may not be extraordinary for you. Even when you both may be perfectly clear about what you want in your ideal mate, one of you may realize that there are missing characteristics or undesirable characteristics in the other person that are not acceptable for an extraordinary relationship. This can be the start of a one-sided relationship. This *does not* mean that there is anything wrong with either one of you. It just means that one of you will not be an extraordinary match for the other. This is where wisdom and maturity play a huge role in making great decisions. There are those in the dating world who are not always honest with their intentions. Words must be backed up by actions. Take your time and be cautious to make sure that your interest and heart are protected.

An interesting dynamic with this type of relationship is that the person who has the least invested in the relationship has the power or control of the relationship. They have the ability to control the direction in which the relationship goes. You cannot will a person to love you or even like you more than they already do. You cannot will or change him or her into the type of relationship you want. This has to be a common desire and shared goal between the two of you. If only one of you is in love and desires a much deeper relationship, don't sit around waiting for things to change. They won't! You need to accept that you are in a one-sided relationship and make the mature decision to move on with your life. You deserve to have your love respected and reciprocated. You cannot have an extraordinary relationship when only one person is giving 100 percent. You deserve the very best, and this type of relationship is clearly not the best for you.

Some people find that they repeat the same patterns in dating and are unable to move beyond the introduction and infatuation phase and sustain a healthy long-term relationship. This can be complex but can be boiled down to a solution by asking a few of the following questions: Do you find that your dating patterns are the same over and over in choosing someone to date? Stop and ask yourself the question: Why? What are the characteristics of the people you choose? Write them down on a piece of paper (or in your journal if you have started one). Compare this list with your list of Must Haves and Deal Breakers. How do they line up or misalign? Have you determined what the attractive characteristics are? What drew you to these individuals? As you answer these questions, are there patterns that start to emerge? Do *you* have personal, self-esteem, or trust issues that need to be addressed? Is your list of Must Haves accurate to begin with? If you are starting to see a pattern in your choices, it is time to break the pattern by making a change in your choices or on your list of Must Haves and Deal Breakers.

Stress-induced decisions

Stress has many forms and faces. If you dislike being alone or are uncomfortable being alone, you may find that you quickly accept dates with those you might not otherwise pick. This can create stress in many areas of your life. We would encourage you to find activities that are group based to fill your time. Be selective and proceed to date only those whom you consider might be an extraordinary match. Not all people are looking for something extraordinary, and most people will settle for something less. This is setting you up for a lifelong stressful situation.

As we have been writing this book, I (Rick) have come across a situation that I have never given much thought to. Many of us like to be or feel the need to be comforters. In a stressful situation, such as serious illness, a traumatic event, or even the death of a loved one, we can find ourselves wanting to come to the rescue and be there for someone in their time of need. In these times of stress, both people can overlook some or all of the natural red flags in order to provide comfort to a dear friend. This is a time when serious emotional connections can be made and eventually lead to serious emotional hurt. For me, this was made clear when a dear friend suffered a tragic loss. My immediate reaction was the desire to be by her side and try to help and comfort her in any way I could. I quickly realized that this could lead to a situation that neither of us would ultimately be happy with, because we would have gotten together for the wrong reasons. Do we care about each other? Absolutely! Could it have ended up in an extraordinary relationship? No, because we didn't have extraordinary connections in the Four Relationship Cornerstones to begin with.

Stress can be reduced and almost eliminated if you find someone you are connected with in all Four Cornerstones and have excellent communication. Stress is a result of an expectation, desire, or need that is unmet. Slow, deliberate dating without sexual involvement removes many of the stressors associated with dating. We would encourage you not to date one person exclusively until you are reasonably sure that you both agree that there is an extraordinary relationship potential that you want to pursue and courtship can begin. Penny talked with a friend who dated singularly for two years and was thinking of marriage. It was an extraordinary relationship, but the family support was lacking on both sides with the children and parents. Some supported the couple and others did not. It created so much stress that they made the decision to terminate the relationship. It was a sad thing for both of them, but neither could or wanted to continue with the family discord that existed. There is no guarantee that when a soul mate comes along in your life, life circumstances won't interfere with the relationship. This kind of family stress can be reduced by preparing the family for your decision and readiness to date. You will be blending families, and all will need to coexist.

Age

Age is one of the areas which we have observed that can create problems in future years in a relationship if there is a significant age difference. It is not uncommon to see an older man with a significantly younger woman and vice versa. While this may seem great and very much an ego boost to have a younger man or woman on your arm, there are some long-term ramifications that should be considered.

One of the initial considerations is that you do not share a "common history." This is a reference to being close in age and being able to share memories of major historical events, music, etc. A significant age difference can hinder certain communications because we have different reference points for making key decisions. If there is enough age difference, there can be problems with family members, such as children. Children can have emotional issues with their parent dating or marrying someone of the adult child's age. Family disputes can arise from the children thinking that the new, younger mate is a "gold digger" —someone who is looking to inherit a substantial portion of the older mate's estate. This is not as uncommon as it may seem. Probate courts around the country deal with estate disputes on a regular basis. Some of the nastiest disputes come between siblings and stepparents.

Next, there are the social situations. Will the new younger/older partner fit in with the other's circle of friends? Again, this can be an issue because of the lack of common history with your friends. Even among friends of the same age, one can feel left out. How many times have we met some new friends only to be left out of the conversation because of a lack of common history? Now compound that by having a significant age difference where historical references, music, etc., create an even greater divide.

Another impact that is rarely considered is the differences that aging will bring. We have each seen numerous situations where the older partner becomes afflicted with age-related problems or diseases in the later years of life. This is a point when significant stress can be added to an already difficult time. Is the younger partner prepared to be a caregiver? Is the younger mate prepared to give up many of the activities or passions that they used to enjoy as a couple? In essence the younger partner may end up alone and not being able to share the day-to-day joys of life because the older partner is too ill or frail to participate. Aging may also bring physical changes that include sexual dysfunction, and these changes can destroy a good relationship very quickly.

Finally, as we age, our interests change. Physical activities and social activities can be diminished by physical and health limitations. With a significant age difference, these changes can lead to discord within the relationship when the changes are significant enough. An example is if the couple enjoyed going sailing and one of the partners decides it is no longer important or they are no longer physically able. One may be ready for retirement and travel while the other may still need to work and is not free to join the other. All relationships are work, even extraordinary ones. When age differences are added without an extraordinarily strong relationship, this can add to stresses that can diminish the relationship.

Respect

Throughout our time doing research and writing this book, one of the common themes we have come across is respect (or the lack of it). When we have listened to couples who have been married a long time, in most cases over thirty years, we have discovered that these couples have a great respect for each other. It is not only respect for their similarities, but also a shared respect for their differences. When you have a mutual respect for each other, you speak differently, you listen differently, and you critique each other differently.

Respect can be shown in many different ways. It can be taking time to cook a special meal, take out the trash, open the door for your mate, spend quality time listening, run an errand without being asked, or any number of other things that may be important to your significant other. Respect can also be shown by things that you *don't* do. It could be shown by not using foul language, not showing up improperly dressed for an event, or not being habitually late.

Men, sadly, in our society today, there is a small contingent of women who frown on some of the traditional ways that we show respect to women. The sexual revolution in society has blurred traditional etiquette, courtesy, and polite behavior. Earlier in this book we told you a story of a man who had been a complete gentleman on a first date with a woman. He opened her car door, opened the restaurant door, helped seat her, let her order her meal first, etc. At the end of the evening he asked if she would like to get together again, and she told him no. He told her that since he hadn't been divorced that long and hadn't been on many dates, he would like to know what he had done wrong. She proceeded to tell him in no uncertain terms that "today's women" are offended when a man opens the door for them and that it is a sign of disrespect. We are here to tell you that most women are not like that. Most women have not been so adversely impacted by "the women's movement." And quite honestly, men, do not take this personally. There are a great many women out there who will truly appreciate your efforts. Sadly, most women are not used to being treated like ladies.

On the other hand, there are women who will wait in the car or by a door for a man to demonstrate respect and courtesy by opening the door for her. Some men are not used to practicing this type of etiquette and it is not second nature to think or behave this way. This same respect can be seen for the elderly. Does your potential date consider and demonstrate politeness to the elderly by opening doors for them, allowing them to go first to be seated, or showing patience in the parking lot as they move slowly? We know this book is about dating, and your date will show his or her true self by being consistent with their manners for all people.

Women, unfortunately there are men who are not trained with good etiquette or manners. They were never raised with the idea that women should be respected. There are men out there who are very self-centered and are only interested in their own personal satisfaction. They only want you around when it is convenient for them. They want their freedom to come and go as they please and to do as they please, yet they expect you to be there waiting on them to call or to come around.

Avoid those individuals with manners that do not match your upbringing or expectations. This is one area in which discord will slowly eat away at you and begin to undermine your relationship. The men and women we have just described should not be that difficult to spot at this point, based on what you have learned. Disrespect and poor manners are red flags that indicate there is not an extraordinary relationship present.

Anxiety of meeting someone new

One of the great barriers to meeting someone new is our anxiety. This anxiety can stem from multiple reasons, including the fear of being rejected, low self-esteem, and the fear of being laughed at, among a few. The greatest progress I (Rick) made in getting to know people was to put myself in a position where I had no choice but to meet new people. After my divorce, I started attending business socials and chamber of commerce functions because of my work. Initially, I felt like an outsider, an outcast, someone who was truly not accepted. After about eighteen months of attending various events, I became reasonably well known and was almost expected to be at each event. Did I meet everyone all at once? No. I would meet a couple of new people at a time and spend most of the evening visiting with my new acquaintances. Gradually, as I got to know people, they would introduce me to people that they knew, and my circle of acquaintances began to grow. While I did this for my business, the process is exactly the same for dating. Expanding your social circle after a divorce or death is important to your success as an individual and in finding a mate. If you have never been married, this is still an important step. You must continually expand your social circle until you find your soul mate.

A great realization that I (Rick) came to many years ago is that not everyone is going to like me much less fall in love with me. This single realization provided me with a tremendous release of anxiety in meeting people. Recall the steps we had you go through in chapter 1 to define the characteristics you are looking for in your soul mate. It would be nice if everyone had the same list, because then it would be so much easier to find a mate. We would all be looking for the same things and have the same characteristics to offer. In the real world, that's not how it happens. We are all different, and we are all looking for different things. So, when you see someone that you are very attracted to, don't be so shy that you lose the opportunity to speak to them. Understand that he or she may not be the right one, but you will never know unless you make an effort to meet them. In business there is a saying: "What would you do if you knew you couldn't fail?" Finding out that someone is not interested in you is not the end of the world. With each "No" you receive, you are one step closer to "Yes"...one person closer to finding your soul mate.

We know that this all sounds much easier than it is. Unless you are a very outgoing type of person, the anxiety of meeting new people, especially someone you are very attracted to, can seem overwhelming. One of the easiest ways to meet someone that you are very attracted to is to find a mutual friend to introduce you. They don't necessarily need to set you up on a blind date. It can be a very casual introduction when you all are at a social event.

Regardless of whom you want to meet and how you decide to meet them, the key is to always be yourself. Don't be intimidated by the person you want to meet. He puts his pants on one leg at a time. She puts her stockings on one leg at a time. What you may be surprised to find out is that he or she may be just as intimidated by you as you are by them. In the end, unless you are willing to step out of your comfort zone...just a little...you may be letting your soul mate slip right past you and never know it.

Marketing 101—where to find a date

So where do you look and how do you find your soul mate? Love is the desired outcome, but you will have to be somewhat analytical to be successful. Looking for your soul mate is really no different than marketing a product or service. You must look at this search as marketing yourself and finding the right target market for what you have to offer and also for what you are searching for. For example, if you are looking to buy a car, you have several choices on where to look. You can go to a new or used car lot, you can look online at several different sites, such as eBay, you can search newspaper classified ads, and or you can use word of mouth, just to name a few. Your search begins by deciding what type of vehicle you are looking for. Are you looking for something practical or sporty, fuel efficient or not, two-wheel drive or four-wheel drive? Does any of this sound familiar yet? You should have already determined the type of relationship you want and the characteristics of a mate that you are looking for, as well as what you bring to the relationship, back in chapter 1.

There are undoubtedly even more options to meet people than there are for buying a car. The point is that you need to understand what you are looking for, and then you can start to determine the best places to look. We have met people who take no active role in their search. They somehow think that the man or woman of their dreams will magically come into their life and all they have to do is wait for a knock at the door. Sadly, the last time this happened was when the prince scoured the countryside looking for the maiden whose foot fit the glass slipper. And even then, Cinderella had to put herself in the position of being seen and found by attending the ball. You will need to look at your list of soul mate characteristics and start to narrow down where you have the greatest likelihood of finding your soul mate. Please understand that, just as when searching for a car or marketing a product for business, you should not limit yourself to just one venue.

Do you live in a small town or a large city? If you live in a small town, you are not as likely to find your soul mate there as you might be if you live in a large city. Living in a small town might mean that you have to look outside your immediate area for prospective mates. Living in a large metropolitan area will afford you greater opportunity to find your soul mate in a relatively close proximity.

Next, what are your interests and hobbies? Joining clubs or organizations that are focused on your interest or hobby can be a great place to start. This will expose you to people with common interests. You may not necessarily meet your soul mate there, but as you get to know the members of the group, you may develop friendships in which you can share what you are looking for in a mate. This could lead to suggestions for other groups that may be beneficial to your search, or it could also lead to a personal introduction to someone who may be right for you. Note: *do not* join groups or organizations for the express purpose of finding a soul mate unless that is the group's purpose. That's just creepy, and you will soon become an outcast of that group. Joining groups or organizations is merely a way to meet people with similar interests. If you happen to find your soul mate there, great! If not, use it as a way to meet people and get introduced to other people through the group. This is known as networking.

Churches are a great way of getting to meet people of similar faith. If you are a part of a strong church family, some of the church members who know you well may know of potential mates for you. Personal introductions can be a great way to meet new people. Many larger churches will even have singles groups that will be focused on social activities for singles. While the goal of the group may not be to create romantic relationships, they are an excellent way to get out and about to meet other like-minded people. This becomes an excellent opportunity to meet someone special.

Business or trade groups are another way to meet like-minded people. If you are a business person, these groups can be great ways to network not only for business but as part of your social life also. Business or trade groups can be very broad or very narrow in scope, depending on what their objective is. Being an active member of a chamber of commerce and attending business socials is a great way to meet and network with people. Many communities will have weekly or monthly socials sponsored by radio stations, newspapers, or local magazines. These are all ways to get out and network and meet other people.

Personal introductions are a great way to meet people. There may be some "safety" in meeting someone through a personal introduction, as the person doing the introducing should know both of you. We have had both good and poor experiences with personal introductions. As with any other form of meeting people, you just don't know until you meet. In these situations, we find it best to chat by e-mail or on the phone first and see what you might have in common with the other person. If you have nothing in common, there is no need to meet.

The bottom line of all this is that you need to first put yourself in a positionto be seen and be known, and second, to be able to meet your ideal mate. If your goal is to date a movie star, odds are very much against you if you are living in a small Midwestern town. You would need to move to someplace like Hollywood and be in the places that movie stars might be. This would take some research and some effort, but it could be done. The point is, you cannot sit home on the couch and expect your soul mate to come knocking at your door.

Internet dating

Internet dating has become very popular in recent years. There are general dating websites that are very large and attract a broad spectrum of people, and there are more focused websites that are designed to connect you with people of a particular faith, race, location, or other criteria. Penny and Rick have both heard great stories of successfully finding a mate and the horror stories of people completely misrepresenting themselves and what they are looking for. Always use caution when meeting someone, male or female, from a website. The key to success with this type of search is to be honest and forthright when creating your profile. In essence, it is a resume of a personal nature and should be written accordingly.

Online dating services utilize photographs or videos to introduce or test physical attraction. Individuals will search volumes of photos to find those who are attractive to them and pass on those who are not visually stimulating. It is one way to ensure that there is a beginning physical attraction before you talk or meet.

For me (Penny), online dating is a challenge because of how people post their relationship status. The great majority of people will post a status of looking for a relationship and for their soul mate. It has been my experience and the experience of many of my friends that this has not been accurate. A better profile posting would be that of casual dating with the intent of a long-term relationship with the right person. Many are not ready for a relationship commitment and are looking for weekend fun, or just to meet someone without any intent of a deeper understanding and commitment. I have found that I can readily identify those who are into casual dating and not long-term relationships. It is done by asking some hard questions that require them to dig deep into their emotions. Casual daters will almost 100 percent of the time pull away or stop calling or corresponding when asked deep questions. Dating should be fun and enjoyable if you have the same relationship goals in mind. Posting a casual dating status is just that—casual. With the posting of a long-term relationship status, you should be willing to dig deep, explore and share your emotions, and develop a friendship with others.

Online dating requires telling your story over and over, and getting to know someone can be exhausting if you let it. Reading profiles is a skill that comes with time. After a while, you will be able to sort through the profiles and know which people will not match up or be a connection. Online dating provides many different ways to express interest. You will learn that you do not have to respond to all those who are interested if you are not interested. Many sites will provide "winks" or flirtations. You do not have to respond to all of these. However, if someone takes the time to e-mail you a nice note, you should respond likewise with an interest or decline. Do not take offense if someone does not respond back or says that they feel there is a missing connection. It can be as simple as "I do not feel that we can connect because I like city living and you enjoy living a country life" or "I have read your profile and do not feel that we are a match." You do not owe anyone an explanation of why you are not interested at this point. There will be those individuals you will need to block from your site if they become overly persistent and continue to badger you.

There is a window of opportunity when you first begin to date. Penny has found that you can ask anything and everything within the first two dates and get a response. A man will tell you almost anything in those first two dates. After that he may become guarded and stop sharing openly. At this point, based on what you have learned in this book, you should know what you are looking for. If your date becomes less communicative about their Must Haves and Deal Breakers, they may be closing down and are not your soul mate. If you help him or her clarify what they are really after in a relationship, you can more fully determine whether this has the possibility of being an extraordinary relationship. Do not take offense if their goals do not match yours. It is not about anything being wrong with you. It is about the timing of life and differences in Must Haves and Deal Breakers. Timing in life is everything, and you may meet your soul mate at the wrong time in your life or theirs. Maturity is important to realize that if the timing is off, it is not destined to be. We have more than one soul mate, so do not give up hope on finding that special one at the time that is right for you both.

Safety and online dating is so very important. Each dating site will provide you with safety advice about not sharing private information, such as your address, full name, and phone number, until you have a safe feeling about the individual you may go out with. Meet only in public places you are familiar with and feel comfortable in. Always let someone know that you are going out on a date with someone you met online. Provide that person with your date's information so your friends or family know who you are with.

All pictures posted should be in good taste, without sheer clothing or nudity. For best results, post pictures of yourself and not necessarily family, friends, pets, or scenery. There will be time later on to share those pictures. Try not to use photos where you are wearing sunglasses. Show your eyes! Use decent quality pictures that have good resolution and that are not too dark, too light, or blurry. Some professional pictures are OK, but because of extra makeup and re-touching, they may not be an accurate representation of what you really look like in person. Use recent pictures, not pictures of your-self ten, fifteen, or thirty years ago. Be honest in your representation of yourself in pictures, just as you should be with your written profile.

Workplace romance

Work can be a great place to meet people, but there should be a caution here for romance. Look at your company policy regarding relationships. One or both of you stand to lose your position and job if you break company policy. Even if you work for a company that has no formal policy about workplace romance, you still need to exercise caution and good judgment. There are a lot of land mines involved with these relationships. Sexual harassment and discrimination are huge issues and can result in some very destructive work environments. Romantic relationships in the workplace can cause discomfort among coworkers. They can cause coworkers to claim favoritism or discrimination. For example, if one person is dating a supervisor, other employees could claim that their fellow employee is getting favorable treatment, or that the rest of the employees are being discriminated against because they are not part of the love relationship. If the relationship does not work out, it can cause significant workplace stress, and co-workers may take sides and further disrupt the work environment. You might want to consider avoiding work romances. Penny met her first soul mate at work. He was a supervisor over her shift operations and work. It was stressful and they both were grateful that she had an opportunity to get a promotion at another company. This happened a long time before there were strict rules and laws governing workplace romance. With today's rules and laws, their relationship would have never been able to be discovered or grow. As we have said, the timing of meeting your soul mate is crucial.

Lunch dating romance

This is a form of online dating that will charge you a fee of around two thousand dollars and guarantee you six lunch dates in the year. However, those who have participated in this type of dating setup complain that the dates that were arranged were people whom they would never pick themselves and there was never a second date that followed. I (Penny) know of two people personally who shared this with me independently of each other, and this has been validated with online reviews of this service. If this is an avenue you choose to explore, we suggest that you proceed with great caution.

Social groups

Social groups can be excellent places to meet people with like-minded interests. The following are but a few examples of organizations or clubs that you can look for to participate in hobbies, exercise, or civic involvement.

Dance clubs, exercise, art, music, or any club with an interest of yours will provide you with opportunities to meet and socialize. Alumni associations and gatherings of professional groups, fraternities, or sororities can provide opportunities to renew old acquaintances and develop new relationships.

Community service groups, such as the Rotary Club, the Lions Club, the Veterans of Foreign Wars, and Kiwanis, are but a few of the national and international organizations in which you can seek membership. By doing a little research online and asking around your community, you should be able to find one or more organizations that you will have interest in and that have a cause you can support.

Other ideas for meeting people are Parents Without Partners or church singles groups that allow you to meet many people in the same social situation and with similar beliefs. They allow you to build your social circle and support group. Remember, you may not meet your soul mate at a meeting, but someone who becomes a friend may have a relative or a friend who may provide you with the connection to meet your future soul mate.

Sports—baseball, volleyball, running marathons, sailing, cycling—are all enjoyed in physically active social groups and gatherings that provide you with the opportunity to meet new people with like interests. You will need to be astute and be willing to make eye contact and then get to know interesting individuals. When you know what you are looking for, it becomes easy to sort through all the individuals to find a meaningful relationship and make connections that are natural.

Bars and nightclubs

Use caution when searching for a soul mate in a bar or nightclub. There are rare stories of people who are successful in finding a soul mate in this environment and social setting, but they are far and few between. Finding your soul mate in a bar is like finding a million dollars on the street or winning the lottery. It is just not likely to happen. Bars and nightclubs are designed for physical attraction and relationships on a superficial level. This book seeks to help you break the superficial connections of the bar and nightclub scene. We desire for you to be successful in finding that soul mate who is extraordinary and who meets your needs in all Four Cornerstones of a Relationship.

Ask family and friends

When you think you have found someone, it is good to consult with family and friends. They are the ones who know you the best, and their opinions do matter. They will be the first ones to see any potential red flags if you are stuck in the infatuation stage. Hopefully you have followed our guidance to this point and this won't be a significant issue, but if it is, be open to their remarks and potential criticism. If you have chosen poorly, it is best to be made aware of it early rather than suffer through a bad relationship or, worse, through a bad marriage. More often than not, you will have to go to family and friends and ask for their honest opinion, because they are not likely to come to you and try to burst your bubble. Ask the question, be quiet, and listen to their response. Do not argue with their observations and try to convince them that they are wrong if you do not like what you hear. Thank them and take into consideration what they have said to you.

Earlier we said not to listen to what others had to say. That was in the context of what characteristics you are looking for in a re-lationship. What we are talking about here is after you think you have found someone, it is helpful to ask for an outside opinion. Your friends and family will see flaws or character issues long before you will if you are not quick to pick up on the red flags that ultimately can damage or destroy a relationship.

The one-hundred-mile rule

Rick was listening to a radio show one morning while writing this book. The morning show hosts had received an e-mail from a female listener asking for their guidance on a dating issue. The young woman had been dating a man for about three months. She said she loved everything about the man except one thing that she thought might be a deal breaker for her. She said her "boyfriend" believed in the one-hundred-mile rule. Rick listened curiously to the conversation the show hosts were having regarding this topic. At the time he had no clue what the one-hundred-mile rule was. I (Rick) may be somewhat naïve at my age but I was amazed at what I heard. The young woman's boyfriend told her that he believed that it was OK to invoke the one-hundred-mile rule. Quite simply, the rule is that when he traveled out of town on business and was more than one hundred miles away, it was OK if he "hooked up"—or, in other words, had physical intimacy—with another woman.

Rick fully expected the co-hosts to make light of the situation, which they did, but then they gave the woman some good advice. She needed to tell her boyfriend that if he believed in the one-hundred-mile rule, then she was leaving him. It didn't matter whether the limit was set at one hundred miles, five hundred miles, or ten thousand miles. The fact that he was willing to cheat on her was the issue, not the mileage. She needed to have some self-respect and walk away from that relationship. He was not worthy of her.

I have to assume at this point that this is more of a guy issue than a woman issue, although I could be mistaken. Regardless, if you are dating someone who is not going to be faithful to you no matter how near or far away they are, you have no business staying in that relationship. Infidelity is infidelity. You need to have the self-respect to walk away and never look back. Obviously there is no significant emotional connection in this type of relationship, so this situation should automatically eliminate that person as your possible soul mate.

Loneliness

We all feel lonely from time to time. We all feel the need for friendships and seek attachment. Without those connections we become depressed and do not thrive. Loneliness is the perception of being alone when what is desired is intimacy or companionship. This is different from solitude, which is a state of being alone. We all need alone time to reflect without distraction. Loneliness is painful and distressing. The intensity of loneliness varies for different personalities, cultures, and backgrounds. For some of us it is more frequent than for others. Emotional separation can result in feeling lonely when in a crowd. Chronic loneliness can result from the feeling of not belonging or being misunderstood.

We all deal with being alone and being lonely in different ways. One of the things to be careful of is sabotaging your success by settling for a less-than-extraordinary relationship just because you are lonely. This is something that is all too common among singles, especially if they are dealing with codependency issues and feelings of inadequacy. There are a lot of different ways to deal with loneliness until you are in the right relationship. It may be as simple as going to the mall and being around other people, going to the library and doing some reading to distract yourself, or calling friends and family to spend some time with them. However you choose to deal with loneliness, don't get caught in the trap of jumping into a relationship just to avoid being alone.

One of the things we hope you discover is that this can be a great time to learn about yourself. Great personal understanding can result from solitude. As we mentioned earlier in the book, it is the time everyone needs occasionally to be introspective and reevaluate what is important and to be sure that you are living up to your values. It is also a time when, rather than looking at your situation and what might be missing, you can be looking at all that you have and giving thanks. This can be as simple as being thankful for clean air to breathe, clean water to drink, and abundant food to eat. This can be a time of great personal growth. It is at times like these that I (Rick) have come to some great realizations, personal epiphanies, and discovered what direction God wanted me to go.

Don't date just because you are lonely. Don't force yourself to date. When it is right, it is right. Just relax and take a deep breath. It will all happen at the right time. You have to be at peace with yourself and at peace with your situation. When you get to the point in your life and let God take over, He will teach you the lessons you need to learn. It may also be that God has lessons for your future mate to learn before He brings you together. It is an incredibly peaceful feeling to let God be in control and not have to worry about what will happen next.

Summary

For an extraordinary relationship to occur, you have to invest time and effort. The bottom line is that you are not likely to find your soul mate by sitting at home on the couch watching TV unless you expect it to be the cable TV person or the UPS driver. You have to put yourself in a position to be seen and to become known. This will take some time and effort on your part and will probably not be quick or easy. You must be selective and not allow yourself to jump into a relationship just to avoid loneliness. Know yourself and what you are looking for and what you have to offer. If you use what you have learned in this book and invest some time and effort, we are confident that you can be successful in your search for a soul mate.

Suggested additional reading

Chapman, Gary. *The 5 Love Languages.* Chicago: Northfield.

Gray, Dr. John. 1992. *Men Are from Mars, Women Are from Venus.* HarperCollins.

Yerkovich, Milan and Kay. 2008. *How We Love.* Colorado Springs: WaterBrook Press.

Bibliography

Adler, F. R. 1998. *Master Dating: How to Meet and Attract Quality Men*. New York: MJF Books.

Braden, Nathaniel. 1988. *How to Raise Your Self-Esteem*. New York: Bantam Books.

Cabot, T. 1990. *Marrying Later, Marring Smarter*. New York: Dell.

Chapman, G. 2010. *The 5 Love Languages*. Chicago: Northfield.

"Dating mistakes to avoid." www.beliefnet.com, April 23, 2013.

Gabor, D. 1989. *How to Talk to the People You Love*. New York: Simon & Schuster.

Goodman, G. and G. Easterly. 1988. *The Talk Book: The Intimate Science of Communicating in Close Relationships.* Emmaus, PA: Rodale Press.

Harper, R. G., A. N. Wiens, and J. D. Matarazzo. 1978. *Nonverbal Communication: The State of the Art*. Wiley Series on Personality Processes. New York: John Wiley & Sons.

Hendrix, H. 1990. *Getting the Love You Want: A Guide for Couples*. New York: Harper & Row.

Herman, E. 1996. *The Romance of American Psychology*. Berkeley: University of California Press.

Jones, K. L., L. W. Shainberg, and C. O. Byer. 1970. *Emotional and Neurological Health*. 2nd Ed. San Francisco: Canfield Press.

Loehr, J., and T. Schwartz. 2005. *The Power of Full Engagement*. New York: Free Press Paperbacks.

Maultsby, M., Jr. 1975. *Help Yourself to Happiness through Rational Self-Counseling.* New York: Institute for Rational-Emotive Therapy.

McGraw, P. C. 2000. *Relationship Rescue: A Seven-Step Strategy for Reconnecting with Your Partner.* New York: Hyperion.

Morad, R. "10 money mistakes that can ruin a marriage." *MoneyTalks News,* October 12, 2012.

Nathanson, D. L., ed. 1996. *Knowing Feeling: Affect, Script, and Psychotherapy.* New York: W. W. Norton.

Nierenberg, G. I., and H. H. Calero. 1993. *How to Read a Person Like a Book.* New York: Fall River Press.

Sofield, L., C. Juliano, and R. Hammett. 1990. *Design for Wholeness: Dealing with Anger, Learning to Forgive, Building Self-Esteem.* Notre Dame, IN: Ave Maria Press.

Ullman, J. 1995. *12 Secrets for Finding Love and Commitment.* New York: Simon & Schuster.

Yerkovich, M., and K. Yerkovich. 2008. *How We Love.* Colorado Springs: WaterBrook Press.

Viorst, J. 1998. *Imperfect Control. Our Lifelong Struggles with Power and Surrender.* New York: Simon & Schuster.